Produced by AA Publishing
© AA Media Limited 2011

Researched and written by
Chris Bagshaw

Additional material and walks by Bill Birkett,
John Gillham, Paddy Dillon, Terry Marsh,
Hugh Taylor and Moira McCrossan (updated
by Chris Bagshaw)

Commissioning Editor: David Popey
Series Management: Sandy Draper
Series Design: Tracey Butler
Copy-editor: Pam Stagg
Proofreader: Ann F Stonehouse
Picture Researcher: Carol Walker
Internal Repro and Image Manipulation:
Sarah Montgomery
Cartography provided by the Mapping
Services Department of AA Publishing
Production: Lorraine Taylor

Published by AA Publishing (a trading name
of AA Media Limited, whose registered office
is Fanum House, Basing View, Basingstoke,
Hampshire RG21 4EA; registered number
06112600)

 This product
includes mapping
data licensed from the Ordnance Survey®
with the permission of the Controller of
Her Majesty's Stationery Office. © Crown
Copyright 2011. All rights reserved.
Licence number 100021153.

A04616

978-0-7495-6905-1
978-0-7495-6917-4 (SS)

Colour separation by AA Digital

Printed by Oriental Press

Visit AA Publishing at theAA.com/shop

A CIP catalogue record for this book is
available from the British Library.

The contents of this book are believed
correct at the time of printing. Nevertheless,
the publishers cannot be held responsible
for any errors or omissions or for changes
in the details given in this book or for
the consequences of any reliance on the
information it provides. This does not affect
your statutory rights. We have tried to
ensure accuracy in this book, but things do
change and we would be grateful if readers
would advise us of any inaccuracies they
may encounter.

We have taken all reasonable steps to ensure
that these walks are safe and achievable
by walkers with a realistic level of fitness.
However, all outdoor activities involve a
degree of risk and the publishers accept
no responsibility for any injuries caused to
readers whilst following these walks. For
more advice on walking safely see page 144.
The mileage range shown on the front cover
is for guidance only – some walks may be
less than or exceed these distances.

Some of the walks may appear in other AA
books and publications.

Picture credits
The Automobile Association would like
to thank the following photographers,
companies and picture libraries for their
assistance in the preparation of this book.

3 AA/Tom Mackie; 7 AA/E A Bowness; 10
AA/Peter Bennett; 18 Stan Pritchard/Alamy;
24 AA/Tom Mackie; 34/34 AA/Tom Mackie;
54/55 AA/S L Day; 65 AA/Anna Mockford &
Nick Bonetti; 70 AA/Tom Mackie; 82 David
Norton Photography/Alamy; 102 AA/Tom
Mackie; 112 Robert Read/Alamy; 130 Alan
Novelli/Alamy; 140 AA/Anna Mockford &
Nick Bonetti.

Every effort has been made to trace the
copyright holders, and we apologise in
advance for any accidental errors. We would
be happy to apply the corrections in the
following edition of this publication.

Opposite: View of Wast Water, Cumbria

AA

40 Short Walks in
THE LAKE DISTRICT

Contents

Walk	Rating	Distance	Page
26 Ullswater	+++	4 miles (6.4km)	95
27 Pooley Bridge	+++	3 miles (5km)	98
28 Gowbarrow Fell	+++	4 miles (6.4km)	101
29 Mosedale	+++	3 miles (4.8km)	105
30 St John's in the Vale	+++	3.5 miles (5.7km)	108
31 Keswick	+++	4 miles (6.4km)	111
32 Caldbeck	+++	2 miles (3.2km)	115
33 Dodd	+++	3 miles (4.8km)	118
34 Binsey	+++	2.5 miles (4km)	121
35 Watendlath	+++	2.75 miles (4.4km)	124
36 Stonethwaite	+++	2.5 miles (4km)	127
37 Cat Bells	+++	3.5 miles (5.7km)	131
38 Rannerdale Knotts	+++	2.5 miles (4km)	134
39 Loweswater	+++	3 miles (4.8km)	137
40 Ennerdale	+++	2.5 miles (4km)	141

Rating
Each walk is rated for its relative difficulty compared to the other walks in this book. Walks marked +++ are likely to be shorter and easier with little total ascent. The hardest walks are marked +++

Walking in Safety
For advice and safety tips see page 144.

Introduction

Choosing where to walk in a place as lovely as the Lake District presents some delightful dilemmas. Do you head west or north in search of solitude, or stay south and east with the crowds? The truth is, if you're planning a walk, wherever you go it won't be long before you're discovering just why it is that this landscape has been considered so special by so many generations.

The National Park

The Lake District National Park protects the heart of the region, a mountainous core with a series of beautiful valleys radiating out from the centre. Many of the valleys contain a lake or two but there's no easy answer to the question 'how many lakes are there?' Only Bassenthwaite Lake in the far north actually formally incorporates the word 'lake' in its name. All the others – and the numbers do stretch into the hundreds – bear the title 'mere', 'water' or 'tarn', ancient words that owe much to the region's settlement by Norse farmers in the 10th century. The same origins can be found for the countless fells, becks and dales that make up this famous landscape.

It is the history and language of the Lakes that has made them so special. Ironically it was not their special beauty that attracted those early farmers, but the availability of grazing land for the Herdwick sheep. The distinctive grey-wooled flocks can be found all over the Lake District, sometimes alongside Swaledales and rough fell sheep, particularly in the east. Sheep farming was developed on a massive scale by the medieval abbeys and monasteries, and the lasting impact of their influence can still be found. Among these walks you'll find sites where the monks owned whole hill farms, smelted iron in the woods, hunted for deer, and, at Shap, built their beautiful abbey in a remote fold in the mountains.

Development in the Lakes

Not everything here is ancient, though the stones you'll find at Castlerigg and on Birkrigg Common above Bardsea can be traced back to the time of the Egyptian pyramids. Windermere town did not come into being before the arrival of the railway in 1847, and many of the district's 'set piece' views owe at least a small part of their existence to the wealthy industrialists of the 19th century. They built their mansions on the lake shores, planted trees and dammed streams. Perhaps most famous of all such places is Tarn Hows, where James Marshall, a Leeds 'wool baron' created his stunning tree-fringed lake where once was bog and open fell.

Opposite: Bridge House over the Stock Ghyll in Ambleside

Of course not everyone was happy with the 'development' of the Lake District in this way. It was natural beauty and sustainable lifestyles that had inspired the Lakeland Poets – in this book you'll keep bumping into the paths of the Wordsworths, Southey, Coleridge and de Quincy. The National Trust has been crucial in preserving much of the landscape, ironically including many of its 19th-century embellishments. Today we would not tolerate schemes like the damming of Thirlmere, the complete foresting of whole hills and valleys, or building a railway up sylvan Eskdale. But the century since these events has been kind, and now they take their place in making the views of the Lake District we come to see. In Ennerdale, the process is now going in reverse and you can discover how the valley and its lake are being 'rewilded' and returned to a more 'natural' state.

So as you walk, you'll be treading in the footsteps of poets and princes, monks and miners, farmers and environmentalists. The scenery is always so varied and there are so many stories to discover, that you'll soon realise that this collection of only 40 short walks is just a taster for one of England's finest landscape treasures.

Using the Book

This collection of 40 walks is easy to use. Use the locator map to select your walk, then turn to the map and directions of your choice. The route of each walk is shown on a map and clear directions help you follow the walk. Each route is accompanied by background information about the walk and area.

INFORMATION PANELS

An information panel for each walk details the total distance, landscape, paths, parking, public toilets and any special conditions that apply, such as restricted access or level of dog friendliness. The minimum time suggested for the walk is for reasonably fit walkers and doesn't allow for stops.

ASCENT AND DIFFICULTY

An indication of the gradients you will encounter is shown by the rating ▲▲▲ (no steep slopes) to ▲▲▲ (several very steep slopes). Walks are also rated for difficulty. Walks marked ✚✚✚ are likely to be shorter and easier with little total ascent. The hardest walks are marked ✚✚✚.

MAPS AND START POINTS

There are 40 maps covering the walks. Some walks have a suggested option in the same area. Each walk has a suggested Ordnance Survey map. The start of each walk is given as a six-figure grid reference prefixed by two letters indicating which 100km square of the National Grid it refers to. You'll find more information on grid references on most Ordnance Survey maps.

CAR PARKING

Many of the car parks suggested are public, but occasionally you may find you have to park on the roadside or in a lay-by. Please be considerate when you leave your car, ensuring that access roads or gates are not blocked and that other vehicles can pass safely.

DOGS

We have tried to give dog owners useful advice about how dog friendly each walk is. Please respect other countryside users. Keep your dog under control, especially around livestock, and obey local bylaws and other dog control notices. Remember, it is against the law to let your dog foul in public areas, especially in villages and towns.

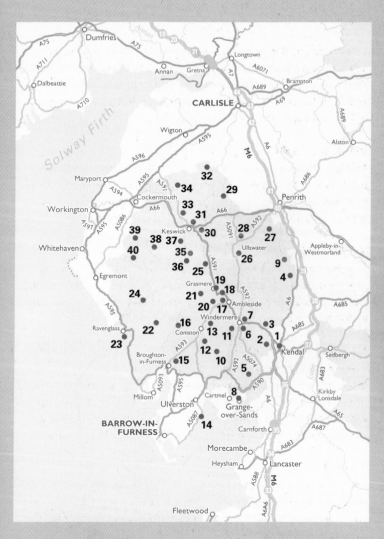

KEY TO WALKING MAPS

⇢	Walk Route	▨	Built-up Area
❶	Route Waypoint		Woodland Area
– – –	Adjoining Path	🚻	Toilet
☀	Viewpoint	🅿	Car Park
•	Place of Interest	🛏	Picnic Area
⌂	Steep Section	)(	Bridge

KENDAL'S TWO CASTLES

Visit two ancient castles,
on opposite banks of the River Kent.

Known as the 'Auld Grey Town', because of the colour of its predominantly limestone buildings, enterprising Kendal retains much of its original character. Sited either side of the River Kent, its occupation stretches from Roman times to the present day and its varied stone buildings, nooks, crannies, yards and castles offer a rich historical tapestry.

Kendal Castle and Castle Howe

Located in a commanding position over Kendal and the River Kent, the ruined Kendal Castle is quietly impressive and offers fine views in all directions. It is thought that Kendal Castle succeeded Castle Howe, sited opposite on the western side of the river, sometime in the late 12th century. After the Norman barons had secured the kingdom, they required quarters with sufficient space to administer their feudal territories and so replaced their wooden motte-and-bailey castles with castles of stone. Timber buildings surrounded by a ditch and small tower were replaced by new stone buildings in about 1220 and work continued until 1280 by one of the early barons of Kendal, either Gilbert Fitzrheinfred or his son William de Lancaster.

Today, the ruins of Kendal Castle consist of a circular defensive wall and three towers plus a residential gatehouse surrounded by a partly filled ditch. The entrance path leads through the wall at the point where a gatehouse once stood. To the left are the largest standing remains, the house where the baron's family lived, known as the Lyons Den, or Machell Tower. To the right, a favourite climb for children, stands the Troutbeck Tower sporting its 'dungeon room' below and garderobe (toilet), with free fall into the ditch/moat, above. If you do climb the tower, and it may be against regulations to do so, take care not to fall through the unprotected hole. South of the compound is a lesser tower and the exit here, a former gatehouse, is now barred by a locked door.

The Parr family occupied the castle for four generations, from 1380 to 1486, when William Parr's widow remarried and moved to Northamptonshire. The castle fell into ruin and much of the stone is thought to have been recycled for use in building works in the 'Auld Grey Town' below.

Opposite: Kendal Castle

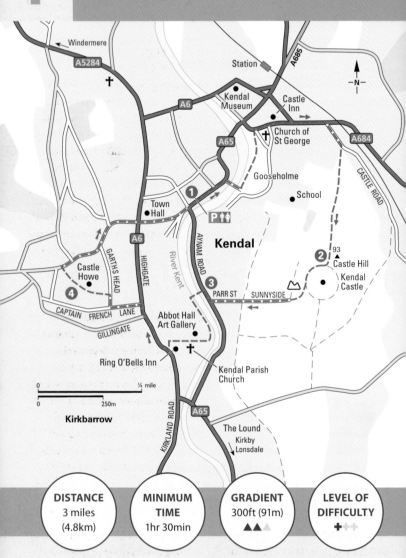

DISTANCE	MINIMUM TIME	GRADIENT	LEVEL OF DIFFICULTY
3 miles (4.8km)	1hr 30min	300ft (91m) ▲▲▲	✚✚✚

PATHS Pavements, surfaced and grassy paths with steps, no stiles
LANDSCAPE Historic townscape and parkland
SUGGESTED MAP OS Explorer OL7 The English Lakes (SE)
START/FINISH Grid reference: SD 518928 **DOG FRIENDLINESS** Parkland popular
but busy roads through town **PARKING** Free parking area by river (occasionally
occupied by fairground), numerous pay car parks near by
PUBLIC TOILETS Near road bridge, Miller Bridge, end of river parking area

WALK 1 DIRECTIONS

❶ Walk upstream along the riverside parking area to a footbridge crossing the river. Cross and bear left to follow the surfaced walkway, through Gooseholme. At the junction of roads beyond the Church of St George turn right down Castle Street. Pass the Castle Inn and Ann Street, keeping right and continuing up the hill to Castle Road on the right. Ascend Castle Road to where a kissing gate on the right leads onto Castle Hill. Follow the broad path up the hill to the ruins of Kendal Castle.

❷ Round the castle ruins until, at a point beneath its southern end, a path can be found dropping down to the right. Descend steeply to pass through an iron kissing gate onto Sunnyside. Go down the road over the old canal bridge and emerge on Aynam Road.

❸ Turn right along Aynam Road to a crossing. Cross and find a footbridge leading over the River Kent. Over the river bear left, downstream, and walk past Abbot Hall to a narrow, surfaced path leading right. Take this path, lined by yew trees and limestone coping stones, to pass between Kendal parish church and Abbot Hall Art Gallery. Emerge onto the Kirkland Road, the main road through Kendal, by the impressive iron gates of the church with the Ring O'Bells pub to the left. Turn right along the road and proceed 150yds (137m) to a crossing. Cross it then bear right to cross Gillingate and keep along the main road, now called Highgate. At Lightfoot's chemist shop go left up Captain French Lane for 300yds (274m), then right up Garths Head. Follow this until a steep path ascends to the left. Steps lead to a terrace and a view out over Kendal. Cross the grass terrace towards the mound and its distinct bodkin-shaped obelisk. Climb the steps then spiral left until, as the path levels, steps lead up to the right to the obelisk and the top of Castle Howe.

❹ Return to the path and go right. Find a gap on the left and emerge on the road at the top of Beast Banks. Descend the hill, which becomes Allhallows Lane, to the traffic lights and pedestrian crossing opposite the Town Hall. Cross the road and go left and then immediately right down Lowther Street. Go left at the bottom to a zebra crossing beyond the Holy Trinity of St George, which leads to the riverside.

🍽 EATING AND DRINKING

Kendal is famed for its many fine pubs and there is a plethora of cafés and restaurants. On this walk you pass the Castle Inn and the Ring O'Bells. Both offer real ale and bar meals. In Kirkland there are several fish-and-chip shops and take-aways. The Brewery Arts Centre, just beyond Captain French Lane along Highgate, has both café and bar facilities.

ALONG THE LIMESTONE OF CUNSWICK SCAR

The heights, extensive views and varied flora, fauna and fossils make this an intriguing and liberating outing.

At the south-western boundary of the Lake District National Park, Cunswick Scar is a high shoulder of white Carboniferous limestone running north to south. Its southern end links with Scout Scar, though a geological fault, taken by the high Underbarrow Road, has displaced the whole of Scout Scar westwards from the northern leg of Cunswick Scar and Cunswick Fell. The effect is dramatic and the tops of both Cunswick Scar and Scout Scar present wonderful views over Kentdale and the Lyth Valley, extending outwards to the Lakeland fells, Morecambe Bay and the distant hills of Yorkshire.

Carboniferous Limestone

The naked white bones of both these scars are composed of pure Carboniferous limestone. This attractive alkaline rock, which has provided the building material for most of the nearby town of Kendal, is home to a rich flora and fauna and noted for its splendid fossils.

By the end of the Carboniferous period the Lake District was buried under limestone. A period of uplifting and folding, followed by arid desert conditions, stripped down through the limestone layers until, finally, the glaciation of the Ice Age gouged, shattered and polished Cunswick Scar principally into the outline shape we see now. The more recent effects of freeze and thaw shattering has added the banks of scree seen to the west, beneath the scar. The dissolving action of carbolic acid, produced by endless rainwater, has resulted in the columns (clints) and deep vertical fissures (grykes) of the limestone pavements along the top of the scar.

The west face of the scar, overlooking the mixed woods, fields and scattered farmsteads of the Lyth and Underbarrow valleys, contrasts with the starkness of the plateau above. On these cliffs, alongside the yew and pine which have forced their way into secure rocky crannies, brightly coloured flowers abound in summertime. In June the prevailing colour of these flowers is yellow. Spreads of common rock rose, hoary rock rose, horseshoe vetch and hawkweeds drape across the rock ledges and look striking against the grey whiteness of the limestone and the dark green foliage of the yew.

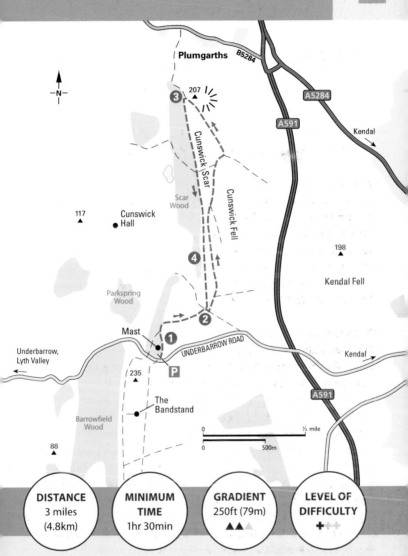

DISTANCE
3 miles
(4.8km)

MINIMUM TIME
1hr 30min

GRADIENT
250ft (79m)
▲▲▲

LEVEL OF DIFFICULTY
✚✚✚

PATHS Paths and tracks, can be muddy, take care as edge of scar is unguarded in places, 2 stiles **LANDSCAPE** Fields and open fell along high limestone shoulder

SUGGESTED MAP OS Explorer OL7 The English Lakes (SE)

START/FINISH Grid reference: SD 489923

DOG FRIENDLINESS Fellside grazed by sheep, dogs must be under control

PARKING Beneath radio mast near top of hill

PUBLIC TOILETS None on route; nearest in Kendal

Cunswick Scar

WALK 2 DIRECTIONS

❶ Walk away from the road, cross the sloping limestone bed that forms the car park and take the track that leads to the communications mast. Pass a low barrier then bear right to follow the narrow path through the wood. Leave the wood by a kissing gate at the junction of the stone walls. Look for a footpath sign 'Cunswick Fell'. Enter the field and continue by the stone wall. On reaching the corner of the field go right and follow the path parallel to the wall. Continue over the humpback of the field and drop to pass a gate, beyond which the wall turns a sharp corner.

🌸 IN THE AREA

To the west of the scar the quiet Underbarrow and Lyth valleys are worthy of exploration. The Lyth Valley particularly is noted for its damson trees. The damson is a form of small plum. In springtime its white blossom resembles winter snows and in autumn its annual harvest is often used for jam or wine making.

❷ Continue ahead on a grassy path for 30yds (27m) then follow it round to the left, aiming for a lone fingerpost. Ignore the right turn and stay with the track over the brow and down to a gate in a fence. Go through the gate and follow the wall on the right as it descends to a dip and round to the right. Beyond the dip, a path traces off left to join a more prominent track.

🍴 EATING AND DRINKING

Kendal is nearby and offers a huge choice. Underbarrow and the Lyth Valley lie to the east and there are a number of quaint little inns that offer bar meals. Nearest to the scar are the Punch Bowl inns at Underbarrow and Crosthwaite.

Turn left on this and follow it to the top of the hill where you'll find the summit cairn of Cunswick Scar, a commanding viewpoint.

❸ Walk on beyond the cairn and drop to the lower terrace edged by the scar. Take care here: the cliff face of the scar is unfenced at this point and reaches a vertical height of around 40ft (12m). Turn left, facing out, and bear south along the edge of the scar. A fence now runs along the edge of the crag. Keep along the rim of the scar through an avenue of gorse and hazel to the edge of a wall. Take the narrow path alongside the wall to find a stile crossing the fence.

❹ Cross the stile and continue by the wall before bearing left to merge with the original footpath at the end of the raised shoulder. Retrace your steps to join the dry-stone wall at its corner, with the gate just beyond. Pass the gate and follow the path along by the walls to the kissing gate at the edge of the wood. Follow the path left through the wood.

STAVELEY'S MILL YARD AND CRAGGY WOODS

How wood and water power brought industry to Staveley.

It's no coincidence that this walk starts and finishes by the modern-day buildings of Staveley Mill Yard. The history of the village and its surrounding area is closely linked to the fortunes of the mills that developed on the banks of the River Kent – there were at one time 30 mills drawing power from the river. This site was once known as Low Mill. There may have been a fulling mill here, processing local wool, as early as the 14th century, but it was wood that really drove the industry on.

Woodlands and Water Power

In the 1820s local entrepreneur Thomas Taylor realised the opening of the Lancaster Canal to nearby Kendal presented an opportunity. The booming Lancashire cotton mills needed vast quantities of bobbins – reels and spindles. Staveley had woodlands and water power to drive machines. Soon he had 24 lathes and four saws, taking power from a waterwheel.

By the 1930s the Staveley Wood Turning Co Ltd was being managed by Edwin Brockbank, himself the son of a bobbin turner. Brockbank became owner of the mill in 1946 and the site is still owned by the third generation of Brockbanks. The company went on to make specialist tool handles, but competition became too fierce in the 1990s and production ceased.

Reborn

So far, the narrative is typical of British industrial growth and decline. The mill site though has been reborn. The coppice sheds, where wood was stacked and dried, now house a number of light industrial units. Other parts of the mill have been redeveloped – cycle and outdoor clothing suppliers, artisan and organic food and wine outlets, cafés, offices and a brewery have all moved in. And up to 15 per cent of the Yard's power still comes from turbines driven by the waters of the River Kent. The coppiced woods across the river are now managed by wildlife charities and the National Park Authority, and Staveley has been reinvented as a thoroughly modern, sustainable community.

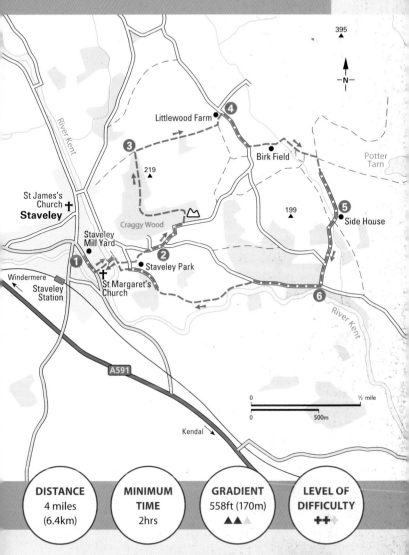

DISTANCE	MINIMUM TIME	GRADIENT	LEVEL OF DIFFICULTY
4 miles (6.4km)	2hrs	558ft (170m) ▲▲▲	++

PATHS Woodland and grassy paths and tracks, road, 6 stiles

LANDSCAPE Village, woods and fields

SUGGESTED MAP OS Explorer OL7 The English Lakes (SE)

START/FINISH Grid reference: SD 470982

DOG FRIENDLINESS Fields grazed by sheep, otherwise reasonably suitable for dogs **PARKING** On-street parking around Staveley Main Street

PUBLIC TOILETS Abbey Square, Staveley

Opposite: Tower of Saint Margaret's Chapel, Staveley

WALK 3 DIRECTIONS

❶ Walk down Main Street, heading south-east to reach the old tower of St Margaret's Church. A footpath runs down the side of the churchyard and along the back of the Mill Yard. At the river, cross the bridge and follow the path beyond to the right. Go through a kissing gate and turn left, staying on the path to another kissing gate and junction. Choose the middle route ahead, and keep a wall on your left through a grove and another gate to a minor road. Turn right to a junction.

❷ Turn left up the hill and, at the first corner, dodge left into Craggy Wood. The single path is obvious and first takes you parallel with the road before swinging steeply up to the left towards the crest of the woods. At the highest point a magnificent view is revealed of the fells beyond. Stay with the path through the woods, as it undulates, trending downhill slightly to emerge suddenly at a stile into a field.

❸ Turn right here, keeping a wall on your left, aiming for a ladder stile on the horizon. Beyond this, maintain your direction across the field, bearing slightly right to find a ladder stile. Continue down the next field with a wall on your left, to a stile, beyond which the wall is now on your right. Keep to this as you descend to Littlewood Farm. Approaching the farm, go through a gate then follow the boundary into the farmyard.

❹ Now join a lane and turn right. Go though a gate and continue on this minor road to reach the access track and a footpath sign on the left towards Birk Field. Walk down the track, then through a gate following the arrow across the yard and through another gate to pass in front of the farmhouse. On the far side join a short stretch of enclosed lane before taking a right turn beyond a tiny beck, then emerge through a gate into a field. The path follows the beck before heading away through a gateway then across a rough field and a gate. Turn right beyond this to join a descending track, ignoring paths left to Potter Tarn, to Side House.

❺ Cross the beck and go through a gate on the access track to join a lane. Heading down the hill, keep ahead at a junction of tracks and stay with this line until you meet a tarmac road at a corner. Keep ahead, down the road, to a minor road in the valley bottom.

❻ Turn right along this for 0.25 miles (400m), picking up a footpath on the left, beyond the sewage works. Pass chicken coops and cross a plank bridge to a stile. A gate by the river leads to a meadow path. Bear right with an arrow beyond a stile and continue on a boggy field route to a gate by trees. An enclosed lane now leads you in front of Staveley Park and past former barns to the riverside kissing gate passed on your outward journey. From here, retrace your steps back into Staveley.

WITHNAIL AND SLEDDALE HALL

The valley and its little reservoir are overshadowed by the cult film made in its dilapidated hall.

Wet Sleddale dam added the valley's waters to Manchester's Haweswater reservoir scheme in 1966, and that might have been the most famous thing that ever happened in this backwater in the Lake District. But in 1985, filmmaker Bruce Robinson chose Sleddale Hall as a location for his 1960s-based tale of two unemployed actors, *Withnail and I*. The valley has never been the same since.

Chaotic Holiday

It tells the semi-autobiographical story of Marwood (played by Paul McGann) and his exploits with the debauched Withnail (Richard E Grant), as the two London-based thespians embark on a holiday in the Lake District. Withnail's Uncle Monty (played by Richard Griffiths and who Robinson has suggested was inspired by his encounters in 1968 with Italian director Franco Zefferelli) owns a tumbledown farmhouse in the hills – Cow Crag in the film, but Sleddale Hall in reality. Their chaotic attempt to use it as a holiday cottage unfolds in a series of witty scenes, now endlessly quoted by students and former hedonists alike. The hall, originally a hill farm, had been deserted, possibly since the 1930s when the Manchester Corporation first bought up properties in the valley. With minimum set-building it was transformed easily into the grim northern wilds of Withnail's imagination.

Film Locations

Other locations include the packhorse bridge (crossed on this walk) where Marwood and Withnail attempt to catch fish with a shotgun, and the phonebox in Bampton, where Withnail tries to talk to his agent.

Ironically the film made little money on its initial release, scant reward for the late George Harrison, the ex-Beatle whose Handmade Films had stumped up half the £1.1 million it took to make. Richard E Grant went on to become a Hollywood star, and McGann became the Doctor in *Dr Who*. When United Utilities put the house up for sale in 2009 it was bought by a fan for over £250,000. It is on private property and is not open to the public.

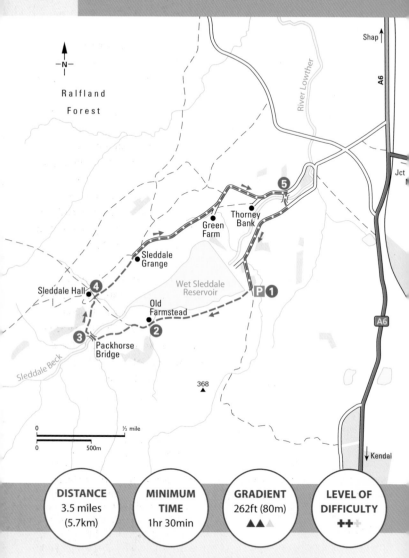

DISTANCE
3.5 miles
(5.7km)

MINIMUM TIME
1hr 30min

GRADIENT
262ft (80m)
▲▲▲

LEVEL OF DIFFICULTY
++ +

PATHS Boggy field paths, track and lane, 1 stile
LANDSCAPE Wet upland pasture and reservoir
SUGGESTED MAP OS Explorer OL5 The English Lakes (NE)
START/FINISH Grid reference: NY 554113
DOG FRIENDLINESS Fields grazed by sheep, so must be under close control
PARKING Car park by Wet Sleddale dam
PUBLIC TOILETS None on route, nearest at Shap village (3 miles/4.8km)

WALK 4 DIRECTIONS

1 Leave the car park by the dam at its far end, walking up a damp track towards a gate by a clump of trees. Beyond the gate follow the boggy track up the valley, ignoring a turning to the left.

2 The track peters out by an old farmsteading near the head of the reservoir. Maintain your direction to a little footbridge and skirt round the edge of a boggy area before picking up a clearer track again through a gap in a wall. The path continues to be damp until you reach a stone bridge over Sleddale Beck on the right.

3 Cross the bridge and climb the bank on the far side following the white arrow to a stile. Turn right, along the ascending track, now guided by further white arrows. Beyond a copse of trees there is a junction by a barn. Sleddale Hall is directly up the slope above you and you can walk around its perimeter, returning to this point. Remember the Hall is private property and there is no public access to the building itself.

4 Go through the gate by the barn and walk along a farm track, now heading back out of the valley. Approaching the farm buildings at Sleddale Grange, go through a gate and thread between a shed and some sheep pens to another gate, emerging on the far side and finally leaving the farm buildings by a gate onto a surfaced road. Follow the descending road for a mile (1.6km), passing through a gate by Green Farm and continuing on through yet another gate down to Thorney Bank.

5 A few hundred paces beyond this farm, a narrow path drops down through to the right and through a gate to a footbridge. Cross the bridge and on the far side join the surfaced road, turning right to walk back up to the car park by the dam.

⊘ IN THE AREA

Shap Abbey, on the other side of the one-street town, is worth a visit. Founded by a reclusive order of Premonstratensian canons in the 13th century, the most impressive feature is the West Tower, added barely 40 years before the abbey's dissolution in 1540.

🍴 EATING AND DRINKING

Instead of turning left back into Shap, turn right and in a short distance you'll see a sign for the Shap Wells Hotel. Hidden away at the foot of a winding moorland road, this venerable hotel has been serving travellers for centuries and is still a splendid spot for a respectable lunch or a proper dinner. There's a bar serving local ales too, with a choice in high season.

YEWBARROW AND THE WITHERSLACK WOODLANDS

A steep wooded climb brings you to a fine view
and a historic manor house, Witherslack Hall.

Witherslack was once owned by the powerful Broughton family. Sir Thomas
Broughton backed the wrong faction at the Battle of Bosworth Field in 1485
and found himself on the losing side. The new Tudor King Henry VII seized his
estates, only to return them again soon after.

Witherslack Hall

In 1487, Broughton rallied to the cause of Lambert Simnel, who was claiming
to be the Earl of Warwick and a legitimate heir to the English crown. Simnel's
claim was supported by a number of Yorkist conspirators and he had landed
at Piel Island, near modern Barrow-in-Furness, accompanied by an Irish and
Flemish army to pursue his birthright. Despite the absurdity (Simnel was
probably of peasant stock and Henry held the real Earl of Warwick in the
Tower of London), the ragbag army, accompanied by Broughton and the Earl
of Lincoln, made it as far as the River Trent, near Nottingham. Here they were
routed by Henry's troops and Broughton was killed. This time the estates
were given to Thomas Stanley, the new king's stepfather, whom he had made
Earl of Derby after the battle at Bosworth. The Stanleys were a powerful
family and as Earls of Derby continued to exert power for many centuries.

All this left Witherslack largely untouched until 1864, when Frederick, the
younger son of the 14th Earl of Derby, decided he would join the mania for
building houses in Lakeland. To his surprise, Frederick became the 16th Earl
on the death of his brother in 1893 and the family decamped to the ancestral
seat of Knowsley Hall near Liverpool. The Hall became a private school, but
Halecat became a family outpost. Michael Stanley, Frederick's great grandson,
lived there until his death in 1990 and the house is still a family home.

Levens Hall

Just a few minutes from the Witherslack is Levens Hall. Famous for its topiary
gardens, this Elizabethan mansion can trace its origins back to the 14th
century. Inside there is panelling and carved woodwork from throughout the
Hall's history, and a campaign bed once belonging to the Duke of Wellington.

Opposite: The Topiary at nearby Levens Hall

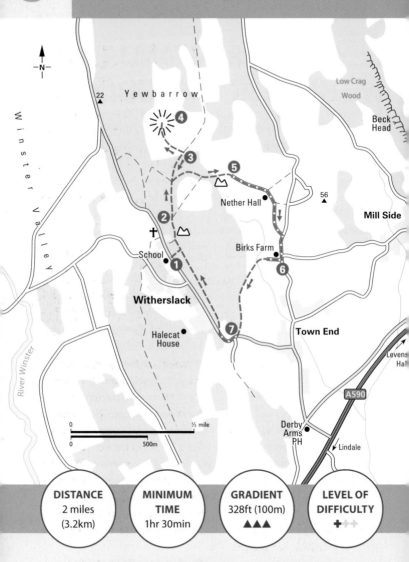

DISTANCE
2 miles
(3.2km)

MINIMUM TIME
1hr 30min

GRADIENT
328ft (100m)
▲▲▲

LEVEL OF DIFFICULTY
✛✛✛

PATHS Woodland paths, farmland tracks and lanes, 2 stiles
LANDSCAPE Woods, field, fell **SUGGESTED MAP** OS Explorer OL7
The English Lakes (SE) **START/FINISH** Grid reference: SD 432830
DOG FRIENDLINESS Dogs may not enjoy the occasional close
encounters with dairy cattle **PARKING** Considerate roadside parking
around the primary school on Church Road **PUBLIC TOILETS** None on route,
nearest at Grange-over-Sands

WALK 5 DIRECTIONS

❶ From the roadside take a short flight of steps up into the woods, opposite the primary school. Follow the path past a seating area, then left, rising to soon join another path from the left. Doubling back, eventually rise to a T-junction with a bridleway, marked by a sign and a cairn. Turn left and continue to ascend through the woods.

❷ As the path begins to level, look for a faint path on the left, through undergrowth. The path becomes more distinct and leads to the village's Millennium seat, with outstanding views. Retrace your steps to the bridleway and turn left. Pass through a cleared area and at a four-way junction walk ahead with the blue arrow.

❸ Soon, go though a gate and step out into the access land. A rough track snakes away to the left, rising gently through a valley. Leave it briefly to take in the view to the west, then cross over to the high ground on your right to get an elevated view of the rest of the area.

❹ Retrace your steps to the gate and the four-way marker. Now choose the left turn, following a path through the woods, your direction soon being confirmed by a yellow arrow. The descent is waymarked down to a stile. In the field beyond, descend steeply, staying with the fence right in a slight zig-zag, before lining up with a hedge to round a small scar and join a track.

❺ Follow this track, through gates to the farm at Nether Hall. Walk through the yard and out on the access track a short way before taking a gate on the left. Walk up the little bank, staying close to the wall on the left to a stile onto a road. Turn right, along the road for 0.25 miles (400m) past a turning on the left, then a footpath sign on the right directing you through Birks farm.

🍴 EATING AND DRINKING
The Derby Arms, just off the A590, offers a range of locally brewed beers to complement excellent food at lunchtimes and in the evenings.

❻ Walk through the yard, descending to a gate at the bottom with another yellow arrow pointing into a field. Follow a muddy track up to a path along the foot of the wooded fell. A gate and stile brings you to another track which follows the foot of the fell. Approaching some buildings on the right, locate a gate on the right and follow the track beside the cottage to emerge on the road once more.

❼ Turn right up the road, following it around a corner, but soon identify a bridleway turn up to the right. Follow this gently ascending route back up through the woods. The terraced path finally reaches the cairn passed earlier, Turn left here, descending the zig-zags to return to the road and your car.

BRANT FELL ABOVE BOWNESS-ON-WINDERMERE

The woods, open spaces and breathtaking views over Windermere contrast markedly with the bustle below.

Walking from the honeypot of Bowness-on-Windermere on a busy summer weekend, it is hard to imagine that just above the lakeside bustle there is a world of quiet solitude and space. Well there is, and this walk takes you there. With relatively little effort you can crest the heights of Brant Fell and enjoy a wonderful view out over Windermere to the Coniston fells and the central heights of the Lake District up to the mighty Fairfield.

Bowness-on-Windermere

Fed by the high rainfall of the Lake District fells, via the rivers Brathay, Rothay and Troutbeck, Windermere is England's largest natural lake. It stretches some 12 miles (19km) in length, is up to 1 mile (1.6km) wide in places, and reaches a depth of 220ft (67m). The Romans built their fort of Galava at Waterhead, on the northern tip of the lake.

Overlooked by this walk, the privately owned Belle Isle is said to have been used since Roman times. Today, this island is supplied by a little boat, which serves the 38 acre (15ha) estate. Belle Isle's interesting circular house, restored after extensive fire damage in 1996, was originally erected by Mr English in 1774. Apparently William Wordsworth accredited Mr English with the honour of being the first man to settle in the Lake District for the sake of the scenery. There have been many more since and it was the railway company that named the station Windermere to attract tourists in the 19th century.

In the late 19th century wealthy businessmen, principally from industrial towns in Lancashire, built luxurious residences overlooking the lake. Many of these private houses are now hotels, such as the Langdale Chase, whilst Brockhole has been the National Park Visitor Centre since the late 1960s.

The Belsfield Hotel overlooking Bowness Bay was bought in 1860 by Henry Schneider, the chairman of the prosperous Barrow Steelworks and Shipworks. Reputedly he left his luxurious home and boarded his steam yacht SL *Esperance*, where he breakfasted travelling across the lake to Lakeside. He then journeyed by steam train, he owned the railway and had his own private carriage, to the works in Barrow.

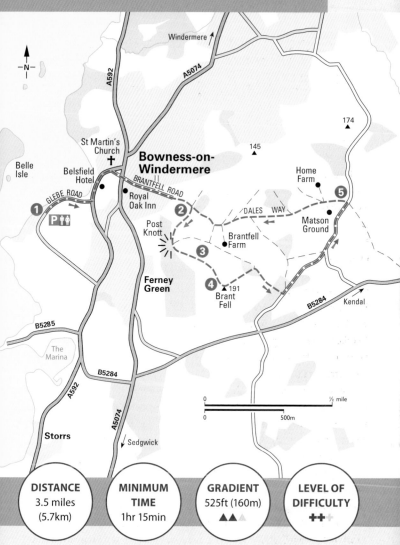

Windermere

A592

A5074

174

145

St Martin's
Church

Belle
Isle

Belsfield
Hotel

Bowness-on-Windermere

Home
Farm

GLEBE ROAD

BRANTFELL ROAD

Royal
Oak Inn

1

P

2

DALES   WAY

5

Matson
Ground

Post
Knott

Brantfell
Farm

3

Ferney
Green

4   191
Brant
Fell

B5284

Kendal

B5285

The
Marina

B5284

A592

A5074

Storrs

Sedgwick

0   ½ mile

0   500m

—N—

DISTANCE	MINIMUM TIME	GRADIENT	LEVEL OF DIFFICULTY
3.5 miles (5.7km)	1hr 15min	525ft (160m) ▲▲△	✚✚✚

PATHS Pavement, road, stony tracks, grassy paths, 2 stiles
LANDSCAPE Town, mixed woodland, open fell, lake and fell views
SUGGESTED MAP OS Explorer OL7 The English Lakes (SE)
START/FINISH Grid reference: SD 398966
DOG FRIENDLINESS Popular route for dogs; busy roads and sheep grazing,
so must be under control **PARKING** Fee car park on Glebe Road above
Windermere lake **PUBLIC TOILETS** At car park and above information centre

Brant Fell

WALK 6 DIRECTIONS

❶ Take Glebe Road into Bowness town. Swing left and, opposite the steamer pier, go right over the main Windermere road and then turn left. Opposite the Church of St Martin turn right to ascend the little street of St Martins Hill. Cross the Kendal road to climb Brantfell Road directly above. At the head of the road a little iron gate leads onto the Dales Way, a grassy and stony path which climbs up the hillside. Continue to a kissing gate by the wood, leading onto a lane.

❷ Pass through the kissing gate and turn right, signposted 'Post Knott', to follow the stony lane. Continue on the lane rising through the woods until it crests a height near the flat circular top of Post Knott. Bear left and make the short ascent to the summit. Retrace a few steps back to the track then bear right to find a kissing gate leading out of the wood onto the open hillside.

❸ Beyond the kissing gate take the grassy path, rising to a rocky shoulder. Cross the shoulder and first descend, then ascend to a ladder stile in the top corner of the field by some fir trees. Cross the stile then bear right to ascend directly up the open grassy flanks of Brant Fell to its rocky summit.

❹ Go left (north-east) from the top of the fell, following a line of cairns down to a kissing gate. Descend through a young plantation to a second gate and a track. Turn right and follow the

> **🍴 EATING AND DRINKING**
> Bowness-on-Windermere is inundated with cafés, inns, shops and restaurants. Conveniently located near the start and finish of the route, at the foot of Brantfell Road, are the Royal Oak and Costa Coffee.

track to a stile and gate leading out to a road. Turn left along the road and continue left at the junction, to pass Matson Ground. Immediately beyond is a kissing gate on the left, waymarked for the Dales Way.

❺ Go through the kissing gate and continue down the path to cross a track and pass through a kissing gate into another field. Keep along the track beneath the trees and beside a new pond, until the path swings left to emerge through a kissing gate onto a surfaced drive. Go right along the drive for 30yds (27m) until the path veers off left through the trees to follow the fence. An iron gate leads into a field. Follow the grassy path, first descending and then rising to an iron gate in the corner of the field. Continue to join a grassy track and go through the kissing gate. Cross the surfaced drive of Brantfell Farm and keep straight onto another kissing gate leading into a field. Follow the path, parallel to the wall, descending the hill to intercept a track, via a kissing gate, and regain Point ❷. Retrace your steps back to Glebe Road.

ORREST HEAD AND A VIEW OF THE LAKELAND PEAKS

Escape from the buzz of the tourist traffic to a nook that impressed generations of visitors to the fells.

It is difficult to imagine, as you stand amid the ever-present traffic on the A591, that before 1847 there were only fields and a few grand houses here. Among those was Elleray, to the north of the Windermere Hotel, through whose original estate some of this walk passes.

A Working Man

Elleray's role in Lakeland's tale is interesting – it was bought in 1807 by John Wilson (1785–1854), heir to a very wealthy Paisley gauze manufacturer.

It was fashionable at this time to have a Lakeland retreat, and the young Wilson built himself a mansion. Wilson had been to Oxford and was of a literary mind, but it wasn't until his fortune disappeared in the speculative hands of a dishonest uncle, that he found he must now work to support his lifestyle. Moving back to Scotland he developed the *Blackwoods* magazine, writing under the pseudonym of Christopher North. Its influence was far reaching. Contemporary contributors included Percy Shelley, Coleridge and Wordsworth, and later the Brontës, Dickens and Poe.

Poets' Party

Wilson spent his time going backwards and forwards between Edinburgh and Elleray. In 1825 he was present at a grand dinner party to celebrate Sir Walter Scott's 54th birthday, held at Storrs Hall, on the far side of Bowness. Storrs was the home of John Bolton, bought with the vast profits this Ulverston man had made through the trans-Atlantic slave trade. Wilson was married to Jane Penny, daughter of the Liverpool merchant James Penny, who was also a prominent slaver. The poets William Wordsworth and Robert Southey were at the party and so was George Canning, Foreign Secretary and soon to be Prime Minister. By way of entertaining these esteemed guests, Wilson organised a regatta the next day, centred around the Ferry Inn. The event was so successful that it was held as a sports day every year until 1861, before it decamped to Grasmere, where it has survived ever since.

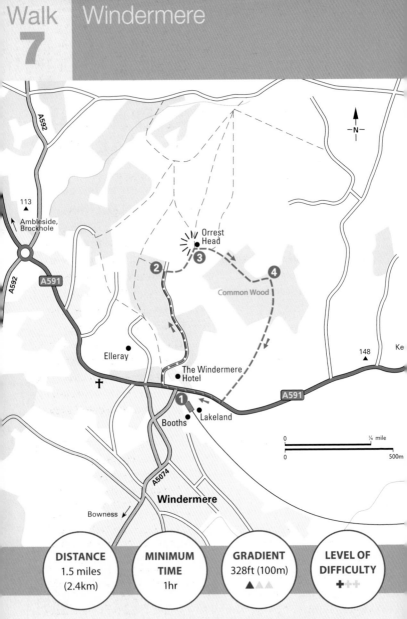

DISTANCE	MINIMUM TIME	GRADIENT	LEVEL OF DIFFICULTY
1.5 miles (2.4km)	1hr	328ft (100m) ▲▲▲	✚✚✚

PATHS Road, grassy paths and tracks, 2 stiles

LANDSCAPE Woods, fields and fell top **SUGGESTED MAP** OS Explorer OL7
The English Lakes (SE) **START/FINISH** Grid reference: SD 414987

DOG FRIENDLINESS Good up to the last 0.5 mile (800m) when they should be
on lead to cross the field **PARKING** Free on-street parking 200yds (183m) up the
A591 towards Kendal, otherwise plenty of pay-and-display parking

PUBLIC TOILETS In Booths supermarket

WALK 7 DIRECTIONS

❶ Walk down the pavement towards the Windermere Hotel, and on the far side locate the large sign to the left with a big finger pointing towards Orrest Head. Walk up the driveway, ignoring a footpath sign off to the left. Instead, stay with the lane, rising up by the hotel and onwards into the woods. The lane snakes its way up the hill, passing a house on the left and becoming a rough track.

❷ Beyond a cottage owned by a wrought iron maker, spot a turning up to the right, parallel with a fence. Follow this up to intersect the track again, below a wall, and turn right along an enclosed track past several benches to a memorial gate on the left. Through this climb the stepped path up to the airy summit of Orrest Head, with its benches and topograph.

❸ With your back to Windermere, walk over the summit past a large bench and locate a narrow descending path through the bracken on the far side, heading roughly due east. Duck below a yew tree as you descend towards woodland and soon reach a wall with a stile. Turn immediately right on a permissive path through a kissing gate into the woods. Follow the trail marked with white arrows through a gap in a wall to a path junction.

❹ Go ahead here, signed towards the A591 and Windermere. Soon, a gate leads out into a field. Ignore the unhelpful and alarmist notice about cattle and walk along the right-hand side of the field. It begins to descend, eventually marshalling you between stone walls, rounding a corner to a gate. Continue on the downward track to the bottom, where another gate leads you out onto the pavement of the A591. Turn left to return to the lay-bys, or right to return to Windermere town.

> ### ⚓ ON THE WALK
> The view is the key to this mini-mountain. A topograph on the summit indicates the names of all the lakes and fells you can see. If it's clear, it is remarkable how the elevated site allows you to see over Claife to the Coniston Fells beyond. They are really much closer than you might imagine from the lakeside in Bowness.

> ### 🍴 EATING AND DRINKING
> There are many options in Windermere town's main street that winds down the hill from the station. A particular favourite is the upstairs café at Lakeland; kitchenware manufacturer whose factory shop is just beyond the station. Here, in a purpose-built gallery overlooking the lake, chef Steven Doherty will persuade you that not all in-store cafés are the same, with a daily changing menu of savouries, ciabatta rolls and platters.

View over Windermere from Orrest Head

OVER HAMPSFELL ABOVE GRANGE-OVER-SANDS

A walk through mixed woods and over open fell above a charming seaside resort.

Grange-over-Sands, with its neat and tidy white limestone buildings, colourful gardens, sunny aspect and seaside disposition has long been a popular seaside resort, particularly since the arrival of the Furness Railway in the town in 1857. Day-trippers would also arrive by steamer via the waters of Morecambe Bay. They disembarked at the Claire House Pier, which was dramatically blown away by a storm in 1928.

Refinement and Open Spaces

Today the sea is somewhat distanced from the sea wall and the town, despite past popularity, has fallen from grace with many holiday-makers and now retains a refined air of quiet dignity. Grange has many fine and interesting buildings and its ornamental gardens, complete with ponds, provide suitable solitude in which to relax and enjoy a picnic. The gardens rise to the open airy spaces of Hampsfell (Hampsfield Fell on the map) via the charming mixed woods of Eggerslack, which add yet another dimension to this pleasant area.

The Hospice of Hampsfell

Built of dressed limestone blocks the neat square tower, around 20ft (6m) high, which adorns the top of Hampsfield Fell, is known as the Hospice of Hampsfell. It was apparently built by a minister from nearby Cartmel Priory over a century ago for 'the shelter and entertainment of travellers over the fell'. Enclosed by a fence of chains supported by small stone pillars to keep cattle out, and with an entrance door and three windows, it provides a convenient shelter should the weather take a turn for the worse. On its north face stone steps guarded by an iron handrail provide access to the top of the tower and a resplendent view.

On the top, a novel direction indicator, consisting of a wooden sighting arrow mounted on a rotating circular table, lets you know which distant point of interest you are looking at. Simply align the arrow to the chosen subject, read the angle created by the arrow and locate it on the list on the east rail.

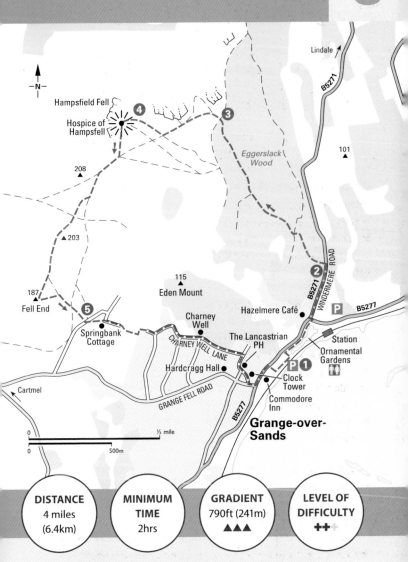

—N—

Lindale

B5271

Hampsfield Fell

④

Hospice of
Hampsfell

③

*Eggerslack
Wood*

101
▲

▲ 208

▲ 203

② B5271 WINDERMERE ROAD

P B5277

115
▲
Eden Mount

187 ▲
Fell End

⑤

Springbank
Cottage

Charney
Well

CHARNEY WELL LANE

Hazelmere Café

The Lancastrian
PH

Station
Ornamental
Gardens

♿

Hardcragg Hall

P ①

Clock
Tower

Cartmel

GRANGE FELL ROAD

B5277

Commodore
Inn

**Grange-over-
Sands**

0 ——— ½ mile

0 ——— 500m

○ **DISTANCE**
4 miles
(6.4km)

○ **MINIMUM
TIME**
2hrs

○ **GRADIENT**
790ft (241m)
▲▲▲

○ **LEVEL OF
DIFFICULTY**
++

PATHS Paths and tracks, may be muddy in places, 7 stiles
LANDSCAPE Town, woods and open fell, extensive seascapes
SUGGESTED MAP OS Explorer OL7 The English Lakes (SE)
START/FINISH Grid reference: SD 410780
DOG FRIENDLINESS Busy lanes and open fell grazed by sheep
PARKING Car park below road and tourist office in central Grange
PUBLIC TOILETS At Ornamental Gardens, north end of car park

WALK 8 DIRECTIONS

❶ Join the main road through Grange and go right (heading north), to pass the ornamental gardens. Cross the road and continue along the pavement to the roundabout. Go left along Windermere Road, rising to round the bend, and find steps up to a squeeze stile on the left, signed 'Routon Well/Hampsfield'.

❷ Take the path rising through Eggerslack Wood. Cross directly over a surfaced track and continue to pass a house on the left. Steps lead onto a track. Cross this diagonally to follow a track, signed 'Hampsfell'. The track zig-zags to the right (with a house to the left) and continues up through the woods to a stile over the wall.

❸ Cross the stile to leave the wood and follow the path directly up the hillside. Pass sections of limestone pavement and little craggy outcrops until the path levels and bears left to a stile over a stone wall. Cross the stile and go right along the wall. Continue in the same direction, following a grassy track, to pass ancient stone cairns and up to the obvious square tower landmark of the Hospice of Hampsfell.

❹ Leave the tower, head south and follow the path over the edge of a little limestone escarpment (take care here). Continue over another escarpment and descend to find a stile over the wall. Descend to the bottom of the dip and

rise directly up the green hill beyond. Cross over the top and descend to find a stile over the wall. Although the path bears diagonally left at this point it is usual to continue directly to the little cairn marking Fell End, with fine views over the estuary. Turn sharp left and descend to pick up a grassy track. This leads left round a little valley of thorn bushes to a gate leading out onto a road.

❺ Cross the road, take the squeeze stile and descend diagonally left across the field to a gate onto a road by the front door of Springbank Cottage. Descend the surfaced track to enter a farmyard and continue left over a stone stile. Go over the hill, following the path that is parallel to the wall and then take the stile into a narrow ginnel. Follow this down, with a high garden wall to the right, round the corner and descend to a junction of roads. Go left on a private road/public footpath, and then bear right at the fork. At the next junction turn right to descend the track and at the following junction go left down Charney Well Lane. When you get to another junction, turn left below the woods of Eden Mount to a junction with Hampsfell Road near the bottom of the hill and turn right. At the junction with a larger road go left (toilets to the right) and pass the church before descending to pass the clock tower and junction with the main road (B5277). Go left and then right to the car park.

SHAP ABBEY AND ROSGILL

The quiet Lowther Valley was once
the domain of an austere order of canons.

The Premonstratensians came to 'Hepp' (it meant 'heap', the butt of many
a Shap joke since) in 1199, from a site near Kendal at Preston Patrick. They
craved solitude and austerity, and by the banks of the River Lowther they
found both. The white coated canons set about building a church and
developing the land around them to supply food and a trading surplus to
fund their work. It was the year the French-speaking King John (reigned
1199–1216) came to the throne of England, and the country would have been
awash with rumour and dissent.

Ambitious Abbot

The abbey building was founded with money from local noble families, and
originally had a cross-shaped plan, with a range of outbuildings you can still
discern today. In the 15th century the nave was extended and there was an
attempt to put up a grand tower over the crossing. There were structural
problems, however, and the idea was abandoned. It wasn't until 1500 that
the plans were revived. Under the instruction of the ambitious abbot Richard
Redman (who went on to become Bishop of Ely), the masons who had
recently worked on the impressive new towers at Furness and Fountains were
engage to deliver a similar product at Shap. Taking heed of lessons learned,
they shunned the unstable crossing and built at the west end instead.

Impressive Tower

The tower, in a typically Perpendicular style of the day, still stands almost at its
original height. Ironically the foundation it served was to last barely 40 more
years. In 1540 the last abbot was pensioned off on £40 per year and became
the vicar at Kirkby Thore near Penrith. Henry VIII's administrators moved
in and sold the estates to Sir Thomas Wharton, the governor of Carlisle. In
the 18th century they came to the Lowther family, and in 1896 the Earl of
Lonsdale removed most of the good remaining carved stonework to decorate
his garden at Lowther Park in anticipation of a visit that year from the German
Kaiser. The ruins have been cared for by the state since 1948.

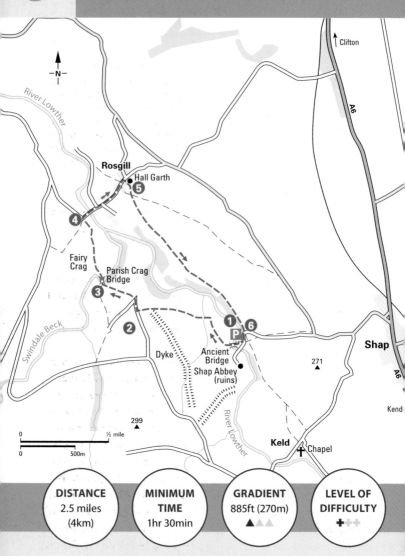

DISTANCE	MINIMUM TIME	GRADIENT	LEVEL OF DIFFICULTY
2.5 miles (4km)	1hr 30min	885ft (270m) ▲▲▲	+++

PATHS Mostly grassy paths and tracks, 5 stiles
LANDSCAPE Fields and valley
SUGGESTED MAP OS Explorer OL5 The English Lakes (NE)
START/FINISH Grid reference: NY 547153
DOG FRIENDLINESS Most fields grazed by sheep, so care must be exercised
PARKING Parking area at Shap Abbey, follow signs from A6 in Shap village
PUBLIC TOILETS None on route, nearest in Shap village (1 mile/1.6km)

WALK 9 DIRECTIONS

❶ From the little car park, walk over the ancient bridge and through the gate on the other side. To visit the abbey ruins, keep straight on here, making for the entrance beneath the tower. Otherwise turn immediately right, up the bank to a ladder stile and follow the riverside path beyond, rounding the river bend before striking off left across the field. A faint field path heads for a ladder stile in the wall ahead. From the top of the stile you'll see the ongoing route, down into a dip then over a shoulder. Beyond the brow the route crosses a medieval enclosure related to the abbey. Look for a gated stile in the wall ahead and the green track leads you onto a surfaced farm track.

❷ Turn right, then as it bends left, leave it for a gate beside some tumbledown farm buildings. On the far side of the old farmyard a stone stile leads through the wall and an indented grassy path leads down the field beyond to a short steep section of path. This leads to the gate at Parish Crag bridge.

❸ Cross the ancient packhorse bridge and on the other side bear right, following the fence around the outcrop of Fairy Crag. Soon you have a wall on your right, and soon you will have to cross a stone stile, which gets very slippery when wet. Stay with the wall at the foot of a bank, soon to reach

a pair of gates. Walk along the farm track beyond which meets a road by a bridge.

❹ Turn right, go over the bridge and up into Rosgill. Ascending the street, look for an opening on the right between Fell View and Hall Garth.

❺ Squeeze through a stile and gate and another gate, then walk across the short field to another stile. Cross the middle of a narrow field to gate. Take the right-hand option of two footpath arrows, and stay on this level field path. Pass ancient farm buildings to another gate and stay on the level route, choosing the left-hand wooden gates when you have a choice. A wall joins you briefly on the right, but it is soon lost again as your route follows the bank top through several more gates. Finally a ladder stile keeps you to the left of an old farm, and you emerge on the concrete access road to the abbey.

❻ Turn right and walk down the hill to return to the car park.

🍴 **EATING AND DRINKING**

Shap has a range of pubs and cafés, especially popular with walkers on the Coast to Coast route. The biggest is probably the Greyhound, a former coaching inn, which serves food in both its capacious bar and restaurant and boasts a large range of real ales.

THWAITE HEAD FELL AND GRIZEDALE FOREST PARK

A gentle walk through forest and fell shows off the many different faces of south Lakes woodland.

This walk takes you through hundreds of years of woodland history, a story that may yet be radically changing again in times of austerity. Beginning in a Forestry Commission car park, you are first confronted by the typical mature conifers of an established commercial forest. The land around High Bowkerstead was already being planted by the start of the 20th century, but it was the arrival of the Forestry Commission in 1937 that accelerated things.

The Forestry Commission
Setting up their base at Grizedale Hall (now an excellent visitor complex with informative displays and shops), the Commission took over plantations that had been created by local landowners even as far back as the 1780s and expanded the Grizedale Forest to cover more than 6,000 acres (2,430ha). Much of this woodland was grown to supply pit props for the coal mining industry, though in modern times it may be used in many other things from paper and cardboard through medium density fibreboard (mdf) to proper sawn timber for the building trade.

Iron and Wood
Back in the 13th century, the woodland here was just starting to be used for iron founding. Monks from Furness Abbey established their iron 'bloomeries' all over this district, smelting iron ore in wood-fired hearths dug into the ground. Dale Park, however, crossed at the end of the walk, was set aside for hunting by the abbot. The dissolution of Furness came in 1537, and from then the woodlands were developed by local landowning families, particularly the Sandys from Graythwaite Hall and the Rawlinsons from Grizedale. Coppicing – the systematic lopping of a trunk to produce multiple growths, was developed around this time to improve the efficiency of the woodland output, and in the middle section of the walk you'll see several areas where trees of this kind have remained. The 'forge' at Force Forge was a bloomery forge. More sophisticated than the medieval versions, it harnessed the power of the Force Beck to drive bellows and hammers.

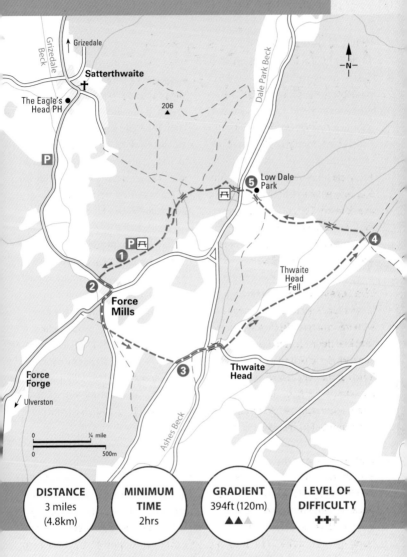

DISTANCE
3 miles
(4.8km)

MINIMUM TIME
2hrs

GRADIENT
394ft (120m)
▲▲△

LEVEL OF DIFFICULTY
➕➕✚

PATHS Forest tracks and paths. 5 stiles
LANDSCAPE Woods, field and fell
SUGGESTED MAP OS Explorer OL7 The English Lakes (SE)
START/FINISH Grid reference: SD 343912
DOG FRIENDLINESS Some livestock encountered towards the end of the walk
in Low Dale Park **PARKING** Blind Lane car park **PUBLIC TOILETS** None on route,
nearest at Grizedale Forest Visitor Centre (2 miles/3.2km)

WALK 10 DIRECTIONS

❶ At the back of the car park, choose the left-hand, green and white marker post for the High Bowkerstead Trail. It rises into the wood and leads you over a shoulder and down to the road at Force Forge. Turn left down the minor road to the junction in the hamlet and turn right, then almost immediately left to pick up a lane opposite Force Mill.

❷ The track bears left to gates into a caravan site. Footpath markers here point the way through the site in the direction of Thwaite Head to the left. At the far side the way becomes boggy to a stile. Beyond this the path steps over a stream then follows the left-hand fence. It's indistinct in places, but worth persevering with through the bracken to descend to a stile by a minor road.

❸ Turn left into Thwaite Head. At a junction turn left then right to the road opposite, crossing Ashes Beck and continuing up the lane. Ignore the first turning on the left on a bend, and continue to a second turning further on. Cross the stile and walk up the grassy track beyond, across Thwaite

Head Fell. Where you have a choice, stay with the central track as the woodland corrals you to a kissing gate. Keep on the right-hand route with a stream to your left and a wall on your right. The route is mostly an obvious groove, eventually passing through a gateway and narrowing to rise up to a stile in a wall. Beyond this you return to the commercial forestry, and through a deer fence reach a junction of tracks.

❹ Turn left, signposted to Low Dale Park, through another gate in the deer fence. Follow the narrow, muddy bridleway through the plantation. Go through more gates, first in the deer fence, then in a wall, to emerge in rough pasture. A green track descends to Low Dale Park, where you pass through a gate and bear right, in front of a green-doored cottage. Walk between the old farm buildings, but before you reach the last one, bob down left following a bridleway sign. The little bank leads down to a road.

❺ Cross over to a stile, then a tiny bridge over a beck by a picnic area. On the far side, a bridleway leads through a gateway and up into the forest. Bear left and plod upwards, soon reaching a junction with a forest road. Turn left, picking up the green and white markers once more. Take the right fork at a junction and stay with the markers at another junction, the path soon steepening to return you to the Blind Lane car park.

> ℹ️ **EATING AND DRINKING**
>
> For daytime sustenance, the café at the Visitor Centre offers a wide range of hot and cold food and drinks. For something more traditional, the Eagle's Head pub in Satterthwaite serves locally sourced produce and good ale and has a beer garden.

CLAIFE STATION AND A PROSPECT ON WINDERMERE

Discover life through a lens in a landscape
entirely created to be picturesque.

Claife's claim to a place in Lakeland history would be secure even if it was
just as the home of the Claife Cryer, a mysterious voice which once tempted
ferrymen to their deaths on dark, stormy nights. Today, the ferry from the
Bowness shore is owned by Cumbria County Council and its somewhat
prosaic roll-on/roll-off service is unlikely to be affected by ghostly wailing.

Ideal View

Thomas West produced a ground breaking guide, *The Lakes in Cumberland,
Westmorland and Lancashire* in 1778, and in it he suggested specific 'stations'
where the 'picturesque' might best be captured. First among these was Claife,
a rustic ferry ride away from Windermere's mansion strewn eastern shore.
The Claife shore had been bought by John Christian Curwen in 1781. Curwen
was a proper industrial magnate, owning huge mining, iron and steel making
concerns in Workington on Cumberland's western coast. The estate included
Belle Isle, where a previous owner had ill-matched the public mood and built
a peculiar circular house. Curwen had grander designs and set about planting
Claife Heights and shoreline with the requisite pine and larch trees that
confirmed his idea of what a view should look like.

On the crag where West had suggested the genteel tourist best captures
the ideal composition of water, farmland, mountain and sky, he built a mock
castellation, complete with glass windows in a variety of shades. One of the
more unusual aspects of this pursuit of the 'picturesque' was the belief that
things looked better if you looked at them in a convex mirror – a Claude Glass
(taking its name from Claude Lorrain, a 17th-century artist whom Gilpin felt
had captured the essence of the 'picturesque'.) Gilpin had claimed that the
Claude glass gives 'the object of nature a soft, mellow tinge like the colouring
of that Master'. Different colour glass brought a different light to the mirror, so
at Claife Station you could admire the view in several different moods.

It seems a strange idea to modern sensibilities, and perhaps unsurprisingly
Claife Station fell into disrepair. The whole estate is now managed by the
National Trust, who are considering restoration plans for the station.

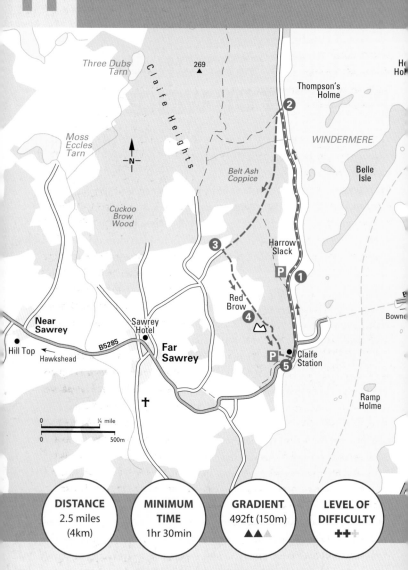

DISTANCE	MINIMUM TIME	GRADIENT	LEVEL OF DIFFICULTY
2.5 miles (4km)	1hr 30min	492ft (150m) ▲▲▲	++++

PATHS Road, forest paths and tracks

LANDSCAPE Woods, fell and lake

SUGGESTED MAP OS Explorer OL7 The English Lakes (SE)

START/FINISH Grid reference: SD 388960

DOG FRIENDLINESS Mostly fine

PARKING National Trust Harrow Slack pay-and-display car park

PUBLIC TOILETS None on route, plenty in Bowness on other side of lake

WALK 11 DIRECTIONS

❶ Turn left from the car park at Harrow Slack, along the lakeshore road, then go through a gate into the woods.

❷ After a few paces turn abruptly left, on a bridleway towards Far Sawrey. The track rakes upward above the Harrow Slack meadows, climbing through woodland. In time, ignore a permissive track away to the left and continue upward. Through an open area, walls close in and you reach a gated junction.

🍴 EATING AND DRINKING

The Sawrey Hotel in Far Sawrey is a good choice. Its Claife Cryer Bar recalls the ghostly voice that haunted the ferrymen, and usually has a roaring log fire. The beer is local and food is simple but effective.

---

❸ Turn left, back into the woods, on a twisting, contouring track passing over a stream before joining an enclosed path. Beyond a wall gap more open country returns, but the way ahead is still clear. Rounding a rocky promontory, the path swings upward to cross the head of a shallow valley. On the far side of this, an awkward manoeuvre around slabs requires extra care when it's wet. The path continues beyond this on the woody ridge before finally reaching the edge at Red Brow.

❹ Here a signpost, buried in vegetation, indicates your direction of descent. The way is steep and winding,

---

🌿 IN THE AREA

It's hard not to resist joining the crowds to visit children's writer Beatrix Potter's rustic little home at Hilltop in Near Sawrey. You can see where she worked, and learn about her role in preserving the local farming traditions, especially the Herdwick sheep breeds. There is more of her art to be seen in Hawkshead at the National Trust's Beatrix Potter Gallery.

---

between tree roots and rocky outcrops. The descent finishes with a flourish at a little rocky pass, which leads to the ruins of Claife Station, fenced off at the time of writing for restoration work.

❺ Beyond the ruin is a footpath junction. Choose the left-hand option, signposted to the ferry and lakeshore. Emerge through a gap in the wall onto the ferry road. Be careful here as the road can be busy. A few paces to the left you will find the Harrow Slack turning on the left. Walk along the road to the car park in 0.25 miles (400m).

🚶 ON THE WALK

The islands on Windermere have always held a certain charm. You can't see much of the house on Belle Isle, but you can see the elegant trees, many planted by John Christian Curwen. The two smaller islands are known as the 'Lilies of the Valley', while in the bay between Coatlap Point and the ferry lie tiny Maiden Holme and Crow Holme.

MACHELL COPPICE AS RUSKIN MIGHT HAVE SEEN IT

An easy woodland trail though lakeside forestry,
close to the home of a troubled 19th-century genius.

John Ruskin (born 1819) came to nearby Brantwood in 1872, and stayed there until his death in 1900. The son of a wealthy Scottish sherry merchant, he had been encouraged to paint and write poetry as a child, and went on to Oxford University as an amateur scholar. While there he began to write about art and architecture, and was inspired by developments in geology. He became a vocal proponent of the works of J M W Turner (1775–1851) – huge impressionistic pieces that had proved unpopular at times, and was clearly influenced by Wordsworth's views of the natural order of things.

Influential Artist

The Pre-Raphaelite Brotherhood, a group of emerging artists in the London of the late 1840s, were also influenced by Ruskin's developing ideas, but personal relationships between them eventually broke down. John Everett Millais even eloped with Ruskin's wife Effie. Her family secured an annulment to her marriage in 1856 so she could marry Millais.

Ruskin was a man of monumental intellect, but prone to appropriately huge changes of mood. He abandoned art all together in the 1850s and wrote about politics instead, developing ideas that would influence the British Labour movement, Leo Tolstoy and even Mahatma Gandhi.

Perhaps it was unhappiness that drove Ruskin to Coniston Water. Certainly much has been written about his sexuality and this seems to have been an area of particularly wistful contemplation. But at Brantwood he settled into a few less pious tasks. He wrote and developed ideas about garden design, heritage and architectural preservation, and put into context contemporary ideas that today we might label 'The Big Society'. Crucially from a Lake District point of view he mentored a number of important local followers, including W G Collingwood (1854–1932). Collingwood studied Lakeland history, becoming an advocate for a view of the Scandinavian influence in culture that moved away from populist images of Viking raiders towards a more benign presence, still expressed through dialect and traditional farming methods. The Ruskin Museum in Coniston owes much to Collingwood's work.

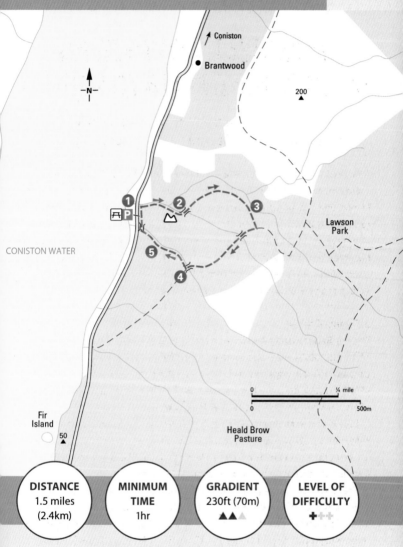

DISTANCE	MINIMUM TIME	GRADIENT	LEVEL OF DIFFICULTY
1.5 miles (2.4km)	1hr	230ft (70m) ▲▲▲	+++

PATHS Woodland paths and tracks, 2 stiles
LANDSCAPE Wood and lakeshore
SUGGESTED MAP OS Explorer OL7 The English Lakes (SE)
START/FINISH Grid reference: SD 309952
DOG FRIENDLINESS No problems
PARKING Machell Coppice car park, on eastern shore road just beyond Brantwood
PUBLIC TOILETS None on route, plenty in Coniston on other side of lake

WALK 12 DIRECTIONS

❶ With your back to the lake, turn right, across the car park, looking for your first purple-topped post. The path leads up into the woods. Initially the going is steep, including sections of steps, but soon it swings away from the beckside, over a rise then levels off. As the going becomes easier, maintain a less steep ascent to a junction of tracks.

❷ Turn right here, to cross a stile and continue up the hill. The purple-topped posts draw you on into a clearing that accompanies a line of electricity transmission poles. The path levels again across the clearing, before descending briefly to cross first a tiny beck then a much larger one.

❸ Ample purple posts lead you into a gentle ascent beneath broadleaved trees to a rough-built hut in the woods.

❹ Just beyond this a yellow footpath arrow tempts you downward, but ignore it. Instead turn right with another purple-topped post amid former coppice stands. Follow the path descending more steeply before levelling off with views across the lake to the Coniston fells beyond. Rising

🍴 EATING AND DRINKING

Jumping Jenny's Coffee House and Restaurant is in an outbuilding at Brantwood. The view from the terrace is as fine as any in the district, while inside you'll find a changing blackboard menu using interesting ingredients, but usually offering a stew, a quiche, a salad and a soup.

again briefly, the path then dips back down towards the little beck and a stile. Over this a purple-topped post leads you on to a wooded promontory.

❺ The obvious route descends to the left, almost as far as the lakeshore before swinging round to the right into a picnic area by the road with a fine view across the lake. Find a little dip across the beck beyond the last picnic table to emerge in the parking area.

⚓ ON THE WALK

Through the woods you'll catch plenty of glimpses of Coniston Water and the fells beyond. The best views though are from the start or end of the walk. Step across the road and stand on one of the tiny beaches that line the shore for a memorable sight across the water, even when the cloud is down

🔎 IN THE AREA

Visit Ruskin's lovely home at Brantwood. The views are exceptional and there are lots of displays explaining the man's significance and his influence in a wide range of cultural and social issues. The gardens are very pleasant too, and you can even catch a steamer across the lake to visit the museum in Coniston.

TARN HOWS AND TOM GILL

A different approach to one of Lakeland's tourist honeypots.

Tarn Hows has been a Lakeland chocolate box attraction since the charabancs first connected it with the railheads at Coniston and Windermere. Its evocative blend of statuesque pines, sparkling water and a backdrop of distinctively pointy fells could have been made especially for an idyllic photo opportunity. And to a certain extent that's exactly how it came into being.

Lakeland Retreat

During the 19th century it became fashionable for the wealthy industrialists of West Yorkshire and South Lancashire to buy a Lakeland retreat. Many of the area's fine houses date from this era. James Marshall was one of these men. His father had built the largest woollen mill in the world, on the banks of the River Aire in Leeds, and retired to a grand residence on the shores of Ullswater (now the Outward Bound Centre). James bought the Monk Coniston Estate in 1835, and set about transforming it into a rich man's vision of the countryside. He created a Lakeland in miniature, which served no practical purpose other than to look beautiful, an aim which most of today's visitors would agree it achieves with considerable style.

National Trust

The whole Monk Coniston Estate eventually came to the National Trust by a peculiar route. It was partly sold and partly bequeathed to them, principally by Mrs B Heelis, who is much better known to the world as Beatrix Potter. She had moved to Cumbria in 1913, after marrying her solicitor, William Heelis of Hawkshead. Heelis had been helping Potter with her acquisition of upland farms, including Hill Top in Sawrey, where the author set up home. The Trust took on the The Tarns (as they were known then) in 1929 with the aid of a memorial bequest from the Scott family and has managed them ever since.

Despite their unnatural origins, this is an important location for wildlife. Designated a Site of Special Scientific Interest, the tarn's sheltered bays are rich in nutrients and the shoreline reeds provide excellent cover for dragonflies and damselflies.

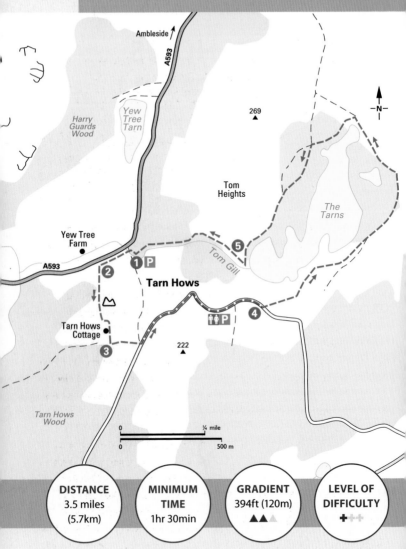

| **DISTANCE** 3.5 miles (5.7km) | **MINIMUM TIME** 1hr 30min | **GRADIENT** 394ft (120m) ▲▲△ | **LEVEL OF DIFFICULTY** +++ |

PATHS Road, grassy paths and tracks

LANDSCAPE Woods, field, fell and tarn

SUGGESTED MAP OS Explorer OL7 The English Lakes (SE)

START/FINISH Grid reference: SD 321998

DOG FRIENDLINESS Fields grazed by sheep, reasonably suitable for dogs

PARKING Tom Gill National Trust car park

PUBLIC TOILETS At Tarn Hows car park

WALK 13 DIRECTIONS

❶ From the car park, facing the road, find a way left through the trees over a bridge and into the adjacent field on a permissive path toward Yew Tree Farm.

❷ At a signpost, turn left, up the hill towards Tarn Hows Cottage. The path is quite steep and leads to a double row of fencing where new hedges have been laid. Go through a wicket gate and continue with yellow arrows and the fencing now on your left. The fence is replaced by a dry-stone wall and the path continues up to a wall corner where it kinks left through a gate and continues up with the wall now on the right. Take the second of two gates on the left and walk past the former farm buildings of Tarn Hows Cottage to a gate beyond a bank barn.

❸ Go through the gate and follow the access track to the Tarn Hows road.

🌿 ON THE WALK

There are many geological features around the tarn – get a leaflet from the National Trust ranger's van in the main car park. Among the highlights are the clear geological fault line, revealed at the head of the tarn and the volcanic debris flow that formed an outcrop jutting into the tarn as a headland near to the dam.

Turn left, ascending the road and eventually passing the main Tarn Hows car park.

❹ Continue for a few more paces to find a gravel track bearing off left above Tarn Hows. Follow the wide track to make an anticlockwise circumnavigation of the tarn. Along the way, theere are some off-shoots giving vistas ver the water. At the end there is a little dam and a gate.

❺ Don't cross the dam or go through the gate, but turn right down the side of Tom Gill, signposted to Yew Tree Farm and Glen Mary. Take the rocky, stepped path down the right-hand side of the beck to pass a series of waterfalls before bringing you out at the back of the Tom Gill car park. Turn left over the bridge to return to the start.

🌐 IN THE AREA

The restored Steam Yacht *Gondola*, built in 1859, was relaunched on 25 March 1980 and plies Coniston Water every summer. The trip starts at Coniston Pier, passing Coniston Hall and stopping at Brantwood, before returning.

🍴 EATING AND DRINKING

There is plenty of choice in Coniston. The Crown Inn does bar meals and is the nearest to the villlage's main car park. The Black Bull brews its own Bluebird Bitter. For a lakeside view try the Bluebird Café by the pier, where the Steam Yacht *Gondola* and Coniston Launch operate.

Vista over beautiful Tarn Hows

SEA WOOD AND BIRKRIGG COMMON

A varied outing to a fine stone circle on Birkrigg Common.

Birkrigg Common is an open expanse of bracken, grass and low limestone scars, rising between the shores of Morecambe Bay and the gentle valley containing Urswick Tarn. There was a chapel here in medieval times, connected to the old priory at Conishead, but nothing now remains except a much later structure, probably built for dramatic affect by Colonel Braddyll when he redeveloped the priory in the 1820s. At the back of the village you should spy the Bardsea Monument, once in the parkland that surrounded Bardsea Hall. This mausoleum to local gentry is supposed to reflect the three families whose interconnection came to dominate the local area: the Wilsons of Bardsea, the Braddylls of Conishead and the Gales of distant Whitehaven.

Geology

The bedrock of Birkrigg Common is Carboniferous limestone. It outcrops only on the margins of the Lake District, most notably around Morecambe Bay and Kendal, but also around Shap and above Pooley Bridge. It was laid down in a shallow sea and once covered the whole of the Lake District, before the area was pushed up into a vast dome by earth movements. Subsequent erosion largely removed the limestone layer, exposing the volcanic core of the Lake District, leaving only a few outcrops of limestone around the fringes.

Ancient Settlements

The area around Birkrigg Common was always fairly dry and fertile, compared to the higher Lakeland fells, so it attracted the attention of early settlers. The most notable feature is an early Bronze Age small stone circle of limestone boulders on the seaward slopes. In nearby Great Urswick, a standing stone, known as the Priapus Stone, thought to be associated with fertility rites, has been forced into a recumbent position at the base of a roadside wall.

A few tumuli are dotted around the countryside and a rumpled series of low, grassy earthworks represent the remains of an ancient homestead site. The limestone has been extensively quarried, and you'll see several remnants of old workings, particularly at the far end of Sea Wood.

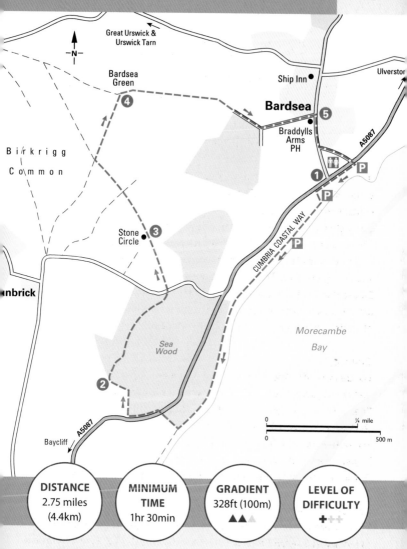

DISTANCE
2.75 miles
(4.4km)

MINIMUM
TIME
1hr 30min

GRADIENT
328ft (100m)
▲▲▲

LEVEL OF
DIFFICULTY
✚✚✚

PATHS Paths and tracks, some may be muddy **LANDSCAPE** Low-lying,
rolling limestone country, with coastal margin, woodlands, open common and
enclosed pastures **SUGGESTED MAP** OS Explorer OL7 The English Lakes (SE)
START/FINISH Grid reference: SD 301742
DOG FRIENDLINESS Under close control on roads
PARKING Small car parks between coast road and shore at Bardsea
PUBLIC TOILETS On coast road below village of Bardsea

WALK 14 DIRECTIONS

❶ Follow the shore along to Sea Wood. At the far end of the wood turn right, up through its inside edge to the road. Cross over, with care, and turn left up the roadside verge for about 400yds (366m). Beyond a lay-by turn right at a gate into another part of Sea Wood.

❷ Bear left to follow a path around the top edge of the wood, then left again to leave the wood at a kissing gate. Cross the minor road and follow a grassy path through bracken above former quarry workings on Birkrigg Common. Bear left where it forks heading gently uphill to reach a wall corner. A few paces further on you'll find the stone circle.

footpath sign at the entrance to a walled lane. Don't go through the gate but bear left with the sign and a wall on your right, continuing across the common. Where the wall bends sharp right, stay with it, now beginning to descend.

❹ At the wall end, go through a gate on the right and follow an enclosed track down the hill to meet a road by some cottages. Continue, across a dip, keeping left at a junction to walk up into Bardsea.

❺ Turn right at the Braddylls Arms (unless you want to stop for some refreshments) and follow the road down towards the shore. A left turn will take you back to the eastern end by the ice cream parlour and toilets.

❸ Keep to the right now, still slightly uphill in line with the wall down to your right. Bear right towards a

BROUGHTON TOWER AND THE FURNESS RAILWAY

A disused branch line makes a fine path above the mosses,
before a woodland return passes a medieval mansion.

Standing in the noble little square at the centre of Broughton-in-Furness,
you may feel there was once some importance to this old Lancashire market
town that seems to have since vanished. There are Georgian town houses
and a fine obelisk, commemorating the Golden Jubilee of George III. Close by
you should spot the ancient fish slabs that once allowed the fishermen from
Haverigg to lay out their catch, and the stocks, where the constable might
detain petty thieves or swindlers.

Furness Railway

In the 1850s the town became the junction between an expanding Furness
Railway, spreading out from the brand new industrial town of Barrow to the
south, and the Whitehaven Railway from the north, bringing Lord Lowther's
coal to Furness's ironworks. A branch line up the valley to Coniston's extensive
copper mines quickly followed and for a brief period Broughton must
have felt like it was at the fulcrum of the new industrial west. Fourteenth-
century Broughton Tower, seen at the end of this walk, had considerable
embellishments added in the 18th century. But industrial wealth is fickle, and
little seemed to stick in Broughton itself.

The railway to Coniston faired little better. Mining traffic tailed off and the
tourist trade became the mainstay, connecting with the Furness Railway's
own pier and the Steam Yacht *Gondola*, plying its elegant way across
Coniston Water. Amalgamation with the London, Midland and Scottish
Railway in 1923, then nationalisation under British Railways in 1948 failed
to address the decline in rail traffic though, and by 1958 it had gone the way
of many rural branch lines. It closed for good in 1962 and the tracks were
lifted the following year.

The 21st century finds Broughton a quiet, attractive country town.
The old railway line makes for a fine walking and cycling route, and the
Tower has been converted into executive flats. The Square is always busy
and the town's market charter is still read out every year. The stocks however,
remain unoccupied.

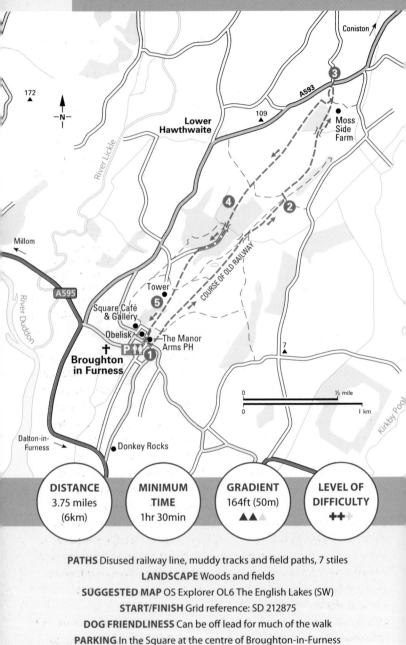

172 ▲

—N—

Coniston ↗

A593

3

Moss
Side
Farm

Lower
Hawthwaite

River Lickle

109 ▲

4

2

Millom ←

A595

Tower

COURSE OF OLD RAILWAY

5

Square Café
& Gallery

Obelisk

River Duddon

The Manor
Arms PH

Broughton
in Furness

1

7 ▲

0   ½ mile
0   1 km

Dalton-in-
Furness →

Donkey Rocks

Kirkby Pool

DISTANCE	MINIMUM TIME	GRADIENT	LEVEL OF DIFFICULTY
3.75 miles (6km)	1hr 30min	164ft (50m) ▲▲▲	++

PATHS Disused railway line, muddy tracks and field paths, 7 stiles

LANDSCAPE Woods and fields

SUGGESTED MAP OS Explorer OL6 The English Lakes (SW)

START/FINISH Grid reference: SD 212875

DOG FRIENDLINESS Can be off lead for much of the walk

PARKING In the Square at the centre of Broughton-in-Furness

PUBLIC TOILETS At south-east corner of the Square

WALK 15 DIRECTIONS

❶ Leave the Square by Market Street. Walk down the left-hand side, passing the garage to an opening on the left and a bridleway sign for Woodlands. Turn left here and join the trackbed of the former Coniston branch railway. Beyond a barrier, the path takes you through a cutting before crossing more open country. After about 0.25 miles (800m) you'll find a tarn on the left with a bench. Continue for another 0.25 miles (800m) until you cross a bridge over a farm track.

❷ Just beyond, look for a wicket gate on the left. Go through it, cross the farm track and pick out a gate on the opposite side. Take the enclosed path, raking upwards, away from the old railway, but still away from Broughton. Follow this through several gates, eventually dipping to cross a pair of becks, then tucking in around a wall on the right close to Moss Side farm. Beyond another gate the rising path passes a treehouse before emerging almost at the main road (A593).

❸ Don't go onto the main road, but turn immediately left down the access track to a house. Signposts direct you around the bottom of the garden and over a stile. Stay on the left-hand edge of the field beyond, crossing a stile and now with a fence left. Approaching gorse, the path tucks in to the wall on the left and follows it around the corner to a narrow stile.

In the field beyond, the remains of an old hedgerow bounds your right-hand side. Maintain your direction along this grassy ridge, go over a stile then descend toward woodland. Crossing a dip you may find it easier to duck to the other side of the hedge to avoid the bogs. Rise to a stile by a sheepfold and continue with a hedge now on your left to the woods.

> ⓘ **EATING AND DRINKING**
> The Manor Arms on the Square, serves snacks all day. Also on The Square is the Square Café and Gallery and on Princes Street, behind the western side of The Square, is the Broughton Village Bakery and Café.

❹ Go through the turnstile and follow a woodland track down to a gate and stile. Walk round the right-hand edge of the next field to a wall gap, then join the left-hand edge crossing a stile to traverse a rise by a knoll. Drop down through a prominent break in the trees to the left picking up a grassy trod, descending diagonally across the parkland. You'll see other tracks homing in on a focus point at a wall corner to the left of Broughton Tower. Keep ahead around this boundary until it becomes a wall and there is a gate and turnstile into some woods.

❺ Stay on this path through a stile and gate and out beyond a football pitch to a larger gate. Go though this, and continue back to the Square.

IN WORDSWORTH'S FOOTSTEPS

Follow the poet through Seathwaite
and the exquisite Duddon Valley.

William Wordsworth loved the Duddon Valley (often also referred to as
Dunnerdale) so much that he wrote many sonnets about it. And little has
changed since his day. There's tarmac on those winding walled lanes, but the
byres and woods and the lively stream that so enthralled the poet are still
there for all to see.

Remote Seathwaite

This walk begins in Seathwaite, a remote village with a rustic pub, a little
church and a handful of farms, set beneath the crags of Wallowbarrow.
The only hint of industry in the valley brought with it a sorry tale of violence
and death. You'll briefly touch on a road that climbs the fell into a vast hollow
below Grey Friar. Here the Barrow Corporation dammed the little tarn to
build a reservoir. The hot summer of 1904 proved too much for some of
the labourers and a drinking session at the Newfield Inn ended in a violent
rampage through the village. Returning to the inn for more drink they found
their way blocked by the bar staff, landlord and others, now armed. In the
resulting fight three workmen were shot, one fatally. The story made the
national papers, but those who fired the shots were acquitted. You'll find the
whole story recounted inside the inn.

Breathtaking Landscape

It's a surprising intrusion into an otherwise quiet scene. The landscape is
still breathtaking, especially if the bracken glows red to blend with the
dusky heather, the crags and the odd lonely pine. The jagged cone of
Harter Fell dominates the skyline high above the forests, streams and
farmhouses. Our route threads through the fields and the bracken. Over
the road, it comes down to the Fickle Steps across the Duddon, which
Wordsworth described in one of his sonnets. It's an exciting prelude to a
wonderful walk through the Wallowbarrow Gorge. From a lofty path you
look down on the river and its bounding cataracts, then descend for a
riverside stroll back into Seathwaite.

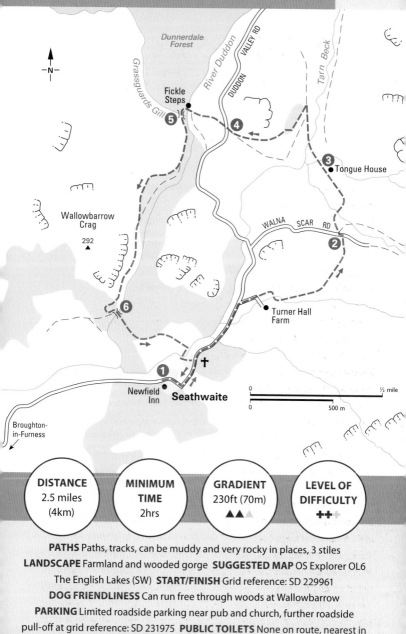

DISTANCE
2.5 miles
(4km)

MINIMUM TIME
2hrs

GRADIENT
230ft (70m)
▲▲▲

LEVEL OF DIFFICULTY
✚✚✚

PATHS Paths, tracks, can be muddy and very rocky in places, 3 stiles
LANDSCAPE Farmland and wooded gorge **SUGGESTED MAP** OS Explorer OL6
The English Lakes (SW) **START/FINISH** Grid reference: SD 229961
DOG FRIENDLINESS Can run free through woods at Wallowbarrow
PARKING Limited roadside parking near pub and church, further roadside
pull-off at grid reference: SD 231975 **PUBLIC TOILETS** None on route, nearest in
Broughton-in-Furness **NOTE** If River Duddon is in spate, it is not advisable to cross
at Fickle Steps; return to Seathwaite along the road instead

WALK 16 DIRECTIONS

1 From the Newfield Inn at Seathwaite in Dunnerdale follow the main valley road past the little church, then turn right on the tarmac lane towards Turner Hall Farm. Leave this and follow a track on the left through a gate marked 'High Moss'. Where the track ends, keep to the left-hand side of the farm, go through the top gate and follow the field path out to the Walna Scar Road.

2 Turn left along the road, then almost immediately, right on an enclosed access track towards Long House. In front of a row of white cottages turn left down a footpath enclosed between stone walls. Beyond a gate keep the wall on your left-hand side, heading for a kissing gate on the far side of the field. A thin grassy path takes you across the middle of the next field to a gate beyond a little bridge. Here a farm track leads you into the yard at Tongue House.

3 Walk through the farmyard and turn left on the access road. When you're level with the edge of the farmhouse garden, take the footbridge on the right over Tarn Beck and up the track towards a dwelling on the edge of the woods. Don't go into the yard here, but turn immediately left, to pick your way across the boggy field. As you approach a barn at the edge of the wood turn right, over a stile and through a gap in the wall. Turn left along a woodland path behind the barn. Continue on this marshy way to the road.

4 Across the road follow the signed bridleway to the Fickle Steps, huge boulders, which allow you to cross the River Duddon. (Caution: if the river is in spate here and the steps are underwater, return by the road.)

> ### 🍴 EATING AND DRINKING
> The Newfield Inn is an attractive pub, dating from the 17th century. There's an open fire and real ales, usually including Theakston's and Jennings, and tasty bar meals. There's a beer garden and dogs are welcome.

5 To continue on the route, turn left, go over the footbridge across Grassguards Gill, then climb on a waymarked path above Wallowbarrow Gorge. The footpath descends again to cross boulder-strewn terrain on the bank of the River Duddon.

6 At a one-arched footbridge, cross the river and keep ahead (not through the gate on the right). Stay on this meandering route over a wooded shoulder and around the bogs before reaching Tarn Beck opposite the church. Bear right here, following the river bank to a footbridge. On the far side turn left in the field with a footpath arrow to a stile opposite the church, emerging again on the main valley road to return to the start.

Opposite: River Duddon

LILIES AND LAKES SEEN FROM LOUGHRIGG

Above little Ambleside, Loughrigg Fell
looks out to lake, dale and high fell.

The favourite of many, Loughrigg is a delightful low fell, which runs from
Ambleside and the head of Windermere lake towards both Langdale and
Grasmere. This circuit walk crosses the River Rothay by Miller Bridge and rises
to a craggy viewpoint before traversing the small Lily Tarn to return via the
stone lane of Miller Brow.

Ambleside

With the exception of possibly thick mist or cloud, this is a walk for all seasons
and most weather conditions. Even before the heights of lovely Loughrigg are
reached, the varied slate stone buildings of Ambleside provide an intriguing
start to the walk. Indeed, despite recent developments, there is a lot more
to this little town than just being the outdoor equipment capital of Britain.
Sited in the old county of Westmorland, Ambleside has long been a site of
occupation. Bronze Age remains, c2000 BC can be seen on the nearby fells and
the Galava Roman fort, near Waterhead, was one of the most important in
north-west England.

How Head, just up the Kirkstone road, one of the oldest buildings in old
Ambleside, is in Above Stock. Sections of this stone house date back to the
16th century and it was once the lodge of the Master Forester of the Barony
of Kendal. It has massive circular chimneys, a typical Westmorland feature,
stone mullioned windows and incorporates stone from the old Roman fort at
Waterhead and cobbles from the bed of Stock Ghyll Beck.

Stock Ghyll once served as the heartbeat of the town when, some 150
years ago, it provided water power for 12 watermills. On this walk we pass a
restored waterwheel, immediately followed by the famous Bridge House, one
of the most photographed buildings in the Lake District. Spanning the beck,
this tiny 17th-century building is said to have been built thus to avoid paying
land tax. Locally it is said to have once housed a family with six children. It
is now a shop and information centre for the National Trust. Ambleside has
become a major tourist resort with shops, hotels and restaurants, and is a
convenient base for exploring the rest of the Lake District.

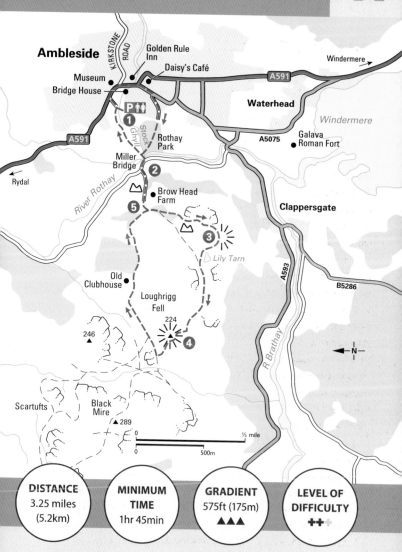

Ambleside

DISTANCE	MINIMUM TIME	GRADIENT	LEVEL OF DIFFICULTY
3.25 miles (5.2km)	1hr 45min	575ft (175m) ▲▲▲	++

PATHS Road, paths and tracks, can be muddy in places, 3 stiles

LANDSCAPE Town, park and open hillside with views to high fells

SUGGESTED MAP OS Explorer OL7 The English Lakes (SE)

START/FINISH Grid reference: NY 375047

DOG FRIENDLINESS Under control; busy roads, park, sheep grazing

PARKING Ambleside central car park

PUBLIC TOILETS At car park

WALK 17 DIRECTIONS

❶ Take the wooden footbridge from the car park and go right, along the Rydal road to pass the waterwheel and Bridge House. At the junction bear right along Compston Road. Continue to the next junction, with the cinema on the corner, then bear right to cross the side road and enter Vicarage Road alongside the chip shop. Pass the school and enter Rothay Park. Follow the main path through the park to emerge by a flat bridge over Stock Ghyll Beck. Cross this then go left to cross over the stone arched Miller Bridge spanning the River Rothay.

🍴 EATING AND DRINKING

Inns, cafés and restaurants and all types of eateries abound in Ambleside. Favourites with walkers and climbers include the atmospheric Golden Rule pub, just up the Kirkstone road above the car park and Daisy's Café, opposite the market cross.

❷ Bear right along the road over the cattle grid until, in a few paces, a steep surfaced road rises to the left. Climb the road, which becomes unsurfaced, by the buildings of Brow Head Farm. At the S-bend beyond the buildings, a stone stile leads up and off left. Pass through the trees to find, in a few dozen paces, a stone squeeze stile. Pass through this, cross a little bridge and climb the open hillside above. The paths are well worn and a variety of routes are possible. For the best views over Windermere keep diagonally left. Rising steeply at first, the path levels before rising again to ascend the first rocky knoll. Cross a stile and a higher, larger knoll offering definitive views of the Fairfield Horseshoe to the north and over Windermere to the south.

❸ Beyond this, the way descends to the right, dropping to a well-defined path. Follow the path to pass a little pond before cresting a rise and falling to lovely little Lily Tarn (flowers bloom late June to September). The path skirts the right edge of the tarn, roughly following the crest of Loughrigg Fell before joining a wall on the left. Follow this down through a kissing gate and the base of a further knoll. This is ascended to another worthy viewpoint.

❹ Take the path descending right to a prominent track below. Bear right to a gate which leads through the stone wall boundary of the open fell and into a field. Continue to descend the track, passing an interesting building on the left, the old golf clubhouse. Intercept the original route just above the buildings of Brow Head.

❺ Continue to cross Miller Bridge then, before the flat bridge, bear left to follow the track by the side of Stock Ghyll Beck. Beyond the meadows a lane through the houses leads to the main Rydal road. Bear right on the road to the car park beyond the fire station.

RYDAL WATER AND RYDAL MOUNT

The tranquil Rydal of Wordsworth and co may be elusive, but it is still a beautiful walk around a lake at any time of the year.

Grasmere and Rydal Water can feel busy at any time of the year and it is sometimes difficult to reconcile the hubbub of the A591 with the land occupied by the Wordsworths and their friends. But such is the scale of this landscape that even here, where the presence of the poet's family for nearly 50 years from 1799 ensures a constant stream of visitors, you can soon escape into a quieter world.

Lakeland Poets

William Wordsworth moved to Rydal Mount in 1813 with his wife Mary, his sister Dorothy and three children. They were accompanied by William's sister-in-law Sara Hutchinson, who was married to Samuel Taylor Coleridge. Meanwhile, their former tenancy at Dove Cottage in Grasmere had been taken up by poet Thomas de Quincy. He soon fell in love with young Margaret 'Peggy' Simpson from nearby Nab Cottage, a little house, now a B&B, you can see overlooking Rydal Water from several places on this walk. The couple were married at Grasmere in 1817, Peggy already having given birth to the first of five children. The Wordsworths and the Coleridges did not approve of this marriage and it became a source of division between the 'Lake poets'.

Poet Laureate

William's most famous works were behind him by the time he came to Rydal Mount, but he was given the post of Distributor of Stamps for Westmorland, largely due to the patronage of Lord Lonsdale and this secured him an income of £400 a year. He spent his time designing the garden and receiving visitors, keen to court his opinion of the once radical poet. In 1843 he was made Poet Laureate. Four years later, his daughter Dora died and William dedicated the field next to the little church he had also helped to design and build, to her memory.

After Wiliam's death the family stayed on at Rydal Mount until Mary's death in 1859. It was his great-great granddaughter who purchased the freehold in 1969 and today, like Dove Cottage in Grasmere, Rydal Mount is a museum.

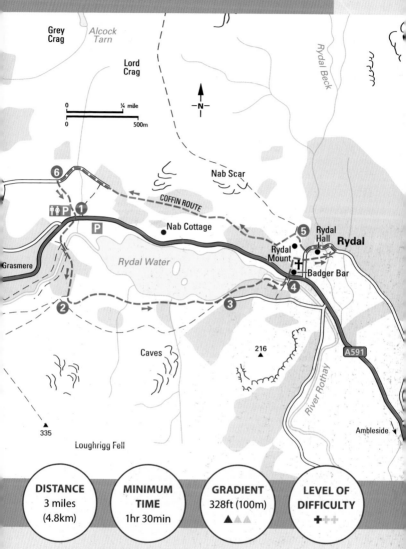

Grey Crag
Alcock Tarn
Lord Crag

0 ¼ mile
0 500m

—N—

Nab Scar

6

COFFIN ROUTE

1

P

P

Nab Cottage

5 Rydal Hall **Rydal**

Rydal Mount

Badger Bar

Grasmere

Rydal Water

4

2

3

Caves

216 ▲

A591

335 ▲

River Rothay

Loughrigg Fell

Ambleside ↘

DISTANCE
3 miles
(4.8km)

MINIMUM TIME
1hr 30min

GRADIENT
328ft (100m)
▲▲▲

LEVEL OF DIFFICULTY
✚✚✚

PATHS Tracks, paths and pavement, 1 stile
LANDSCAPE Woods, field, fell and lake
SUGGESTED MAP OS Explorer OL7 The English Lakes (SE)
START/FINISH Grid reference: NY 349065 **DOG FRIENDLINESS** Can be off lead in woods, but should be under close control elsewhere, especially in Rydal village and among sheep on Coffin Route **PARKING** White Moss pay-and-display car park
PUBLIC TOILETS At car park

Opposite: View over Rydal Water

WALK 18 DIRECTIONS

❶ Leave the lower White Moss car park and continue on the riverside path through meadows to a bridge over the river. Cross the bridge and keep straight ahead into the woods beyond. The path rises gradually, eventually stepping up to a narrow stile in a wall.

❷ Go through this and turn left down the hill on a broad path with a wall to your left. A set of boulders help you over a tiny beck and you continue down. Eventually the path narrows and becomes briefly enclosed before you emerge on the shore of Rydal Water. Walk along the lakeshore path, rounding a craggy section before continuing on to a junction. Stay with the lakeside option, aiming for a gate.

❸ Beyond, walk through the woods on the obvious path which in time leads to a kissing gate and a path through a field at the foot of the lake. With the River Rothay now on your left, head for a footbridge. Cross it and walk up the ramp on the far side to emerge on the pavement by the main A591.

❹ Cross the road with care and pass Badger Bar and the entrance to Dora's Field. At the junction, turn left up the hill towards Rydal Mount, passing the church on the left. Opposite the last gate into the churchyard, go through a gateway on the right into the grounds of Rydal Manor. (If the Rydal Manor grounds are closed, you can continue the walk by staying on the lane here up to Rydal Mount.) A permissive path leads you up through the gardens. Turn right at a junction to pass in front of the house up to the left and the Quiet Garden to the right. Over the bridge you catch a glimpse of the waterfall and its Grot (grotto). Turn left beyond to recross the beck and pass the tea room following the access road out of the estate and back to the lane. Turn right, steeply up the hill.

❺ Beyond a signpost on the left points you along a side lane to join the Coffin Route. Go through the gate and follow the track. Beyond Wordsworth's garden a gate leads you out onto hillside and the undulating path ahead is clear. Through several gates it continues for just over a mile (1.6km) until you reach a junction below a cottage.

❻ Go through a gate and turn left down a track. Beyond a gate enter a wooded area with a waterfall right. Continue down to emerge again on the A591 close to the White Moss car park. Cross to return to the lower car park or turn right for the upper area.

ⓦ EATING AND DRINKING

The Badger Bar at the Rothay Glen Hotel is a firm favourite with walkers, being next door to Dora's Field and possessing a pleasant garden. Both the food and the beer are reliable and tasty. At Rydal Hall the Old Schoolhouse Tearoom serves light lunches and cakes.

ALCOCK TARN

A steep ascent in the footsteps of poets and runners, leads to a moorland tarn, some fine views and finally Dove Cottage.

Dove Cottage, home to William Wordsworth and his family, was known to the poet as Town End and had formerly been an ale house called the Dove and Olive Bough. The Wordsworths arrived here on foot, just before Christmas in 1799. They paid £8 a year in rent and left nine years later for a variety of homes before ending up a few miles away at Rydal in 1813.

Wordsworth's Lake District

Today, Dove Cottage is a complex of academic and artistic endeavours as well as a museum, art gallery and tea room. This walk ends by the latest addition, the Jerwood Centre, opened in 2005 by poet Seamus Heaney. It houses an academic reading room for the Wordsworth Trust's collection of historic manuscripts. It's fair to say that the Wordsworths would probably not recognise this as the same place that William settled in to write 'Daffodils'.

Some things may be familiar though. The mercilessly steep section of this walk that leads from the back of Forest Side and takes you up into Greenhead Gill, is still perhaps as stiff a climb as Wordsworth remembered it in his poem 'Michael': *'his feet struggling in such bold ascent'*.

Missing from the gill in Wordsworth's day would have been the parapet of the Thirlmere aqueduct and associated pieces of water supply equipment but the 'pastoral mountains still front you face to face'.

Another addition is the tarn in the hollow beneath Butter Crag. Alcock Tarn was once a boggy depression and took its name from the rocks that rise above on the slopes of Heron Pike. Mr Alcock of the Hollins in the valley below enlarged it with a dam and stocked it with trout at the end of the 19th century. Alcock Tarn was bought, along with much of the fell, by the National Trust in the 1940s.

Also, look out for the little flourish of crag that marks your descent route known as Grey Crag. It is the destination of the Guides Race at the annual Grasmere Sports, held late August, the runners taking the direct route from the Sports field up the steep field below the fell and back again. The record for the seniors' race is just over 12 minutes!

DISTANCE
3 miles
(4.8km)

MINIMUM TIME
2hrs

GRADIENT
984ft (300m)
▲▲▲

LEVEL OF DIFFICULTY
+++

PATHS Road, grassy paths and tracks
LANDSCAPE Woods, field, fell, tarn and lake
SUGGESTED MAP OS Explorer OL7 The English Lakes (SE)
START/FINISH Grid reference: NY 339072 **DOG FRIENDLINESS** Some places
grazed by sheep **PARKING** Grasmere National Park Authority pay-and-display
car park by the sports ground on the southern side of the village
PUBLIC TOILETS At car park

WALK 19 DIRECTIONS

❶ From the far end of the car park, close to the toilets, locate a snicket round the back of the school and follow it, turning right at a junction and passing the old Workman's Reading Room. Keep ahead at a crossing of paths by a small bridge and go through a kissing gate to join a meadow path. It bears to the left of a stand of pines and meanders its way through several gates to reach the main road.

❷ Turn left along the pavement for a few paces, before crossing over to the lane adjacent to the Catholic church. Walk up this quiet residential lane, staying with it as it swings round to the left. At a junction, turn right and continue until a footpath sign on the right points you up towards Alcock Tarn. At the top of this lane, go through a gate onto the open fell.

❸ Turn immediately right over a little bridge to walk up the right-hand side of the beck as you look up. The path ascends steeply and is paved in places, at the side of a plantation. Beyond a bench, keep going upwards. The slope lessens momentarily to round the head of a wall before cutting back to continue zig-zagging up the hill. A line of crags fills your immediate horizon until you work your way beyond them, swinging round to the right and levelling off, though the tarn remains hidden. A wall joins you on one side and a gate takes you through a crossing wall. Passing several little boggy tarnlets you go through another gate to reach Alcock Tarn.

❹ Half-way along, a little bluff on the right affords great views of the valley below. Pass the tarn and its dam and take the right fork, aiming for a gap in the wall. A way now descends beside the rocky promontory of Grey Crag, a zig-zag path beginning just beneath the crag itself. The descent is steep and rocky in places but navigation is fairly straightforward, keeping to an engineered route down to a gate. Through this the descent continues past a bench and a little reservoir by a stand of trees. At a junction of tracks keep left, above a plantation. Go through a metal gate into the woods and you soon reach a second gate.

❺ Keep ahead around the grounds of Wood Close, descending to a lane. Don't go out onto the lane, but turn right, descending on a track that emerges at Woodland Crag Cottage. Turn left along the access road and left again with a tarmac lane. After a few paces a right-hand dodge cuts off the corner down to a road. Turn right, and eventually right again at the road by a coffin resting stone. Emerge at Dove Cottage, walking past the museum and gallery to the main road.

❻ Turn right to cross beyond the mini-roundabout, then follow the road back toward Grasmere and the car park.

FOUR SEASONS BY ELTER WATER AND LOUGHRIGG TARN

Bluebell woods, a lake, a tarn, a waterfall and Little Loughrigg make this a memorable outing.

Although it does include steep sections of ascent and descent this is not a desperately difficult walk. There are outstanding views throughout its length. The little lake of Elter Water and the petite Loughrigg Tarn are among the prettiest stretches of water in the region. The former, really three interconnected basins, was originally named Eltermere, which translates directly from the Old Norse (Viking) into 'swan lake'. The swans are still here in abundance. Be careful they don't grab your sandwiches should you choose to eat your lunch on the wooden bench at the foot of the lake. The views over both lake and tarn to the reclining lion profile of the Langdale Pikes are particularly evocative.

This is very much a walk for all seasons, and should the section through the meadows by the Brathay be flooded, then a simple detour can easily be made on to the road to bypass the problem.

Local Gunpowder Works

With all the quarrying and mining that once took place in the Lake District, including a little poaching for the pot, there used to be a considerable demand for 'black powder' or gunpowder. Elterwater Gunpowder Works, founded in 1824, once filled that demand. The natural water power of Langdale Beck was utilised to drive great grinding wheels or millstones. Prime quality charcoal came from the local coppices, whilst saltpetre and sulphur were imported. In the 1890s the works employed around 80 people. Accidental explosions did occur, notably in 1916 when four men were killed. The whole enterprise closed down in 1929. Today the site is occupied by the highly desirable Langdale Timeshare organisation, with only the massive mill wheels on display to bear witness to times past.

Of course, the ingredients had to be brought in and the gunpowder taken away by horse and cart. Clydesdales were preferred for their huge strength and intelligence. On workdays they would be harnessed up and on special occasions they were decorated with horse brasses. The horses have long gone but some of their brasses remain fixed to the beams in the Brittania Inn.

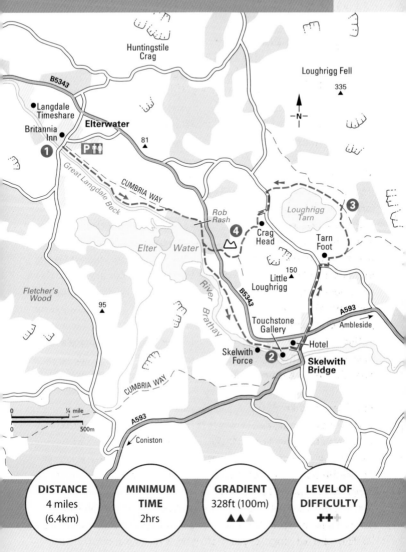

DISTANCE	**MINIMUM TIME**	**GRADIENT**	**LEVEL OF DIFFICULTY**
4 miles (6.4km)	2hrs	328ft (100m) ▲▲▲	++ +

PATHS Grassy and stony paths and tracks, surfaced lane, 4 stiles
LANDSCAPE Lake, tarn, fields, woods, open fellside, views to fells
SUGGESTED MAP OS Explorer OL7 The English Lakes (SE)
START/FINISH Grid reference: NY 328048
DOG FRIENDLINESS Under control at all time; fellside grazed by sheep
PARKING National Trust pay-and-display car park at Elterwater village
PUBLIC TOILETS Above car park in Elterwater village

WALK 20 DIRECTIONS

1 Pass through a small gate to walk downsteam above Great Langdale Beck. Continue to enter the mixed woods of Rob Rash. A little gate leads through the stone wall; the open foot of Elter Water lies to the right. Continue along the path through the meadows above the river. Note that this section can be wet and is prone to flooding. Pass through the gate and enter mixed woods. Keep along the path to pass Skelwith Force waterfall down to the right. A little bridge leads across a channel to a viewing point above the falls. Keep along the path to pass between industrial buildings belonging to Kirkstone Quarry.

2 Touchstone Gallery is on the right, as the path becomes a small surfaced road. Continue to intercept the A593 by the bridge over the river, where there are picnic benches. Turn left to pass the hotel. At the road junction, cross over the Great Langdale road to a lane that passes by the end of the cottages. Follow the lane, ascending to intercept another road. Turn right for a short distance and then left towards Tarn Foot farm. Bear right along the track, in front of the cottages. Where the track splits, bear left. Through the gate carry on along the track to overlook Loughrigg Tarn. At a point half-way along the tarn cross the stile over the iron railings on the left.

3 Follow the footpath down the meadow to traverse right, just above the tarn. The footpath swings off right to climb a ladder stile over the stone wall. Follow the grassy track leading right, up the hill, to a gate and stile on to the road. Turn left along the road, until a surfaced drive leads up to the right, signed 'Public Footpath Skelwith Bridge'. Pass a small cottage and keep on the track to pass a higher cottage, Crag Head. A little way above this, a narrow grassy footpath leads off right, up the hillside, to gain a level shoulder between the craggy outcrops of Little Loughrigg.

4 Cross the shoulder and descend the path, passing a tarnlet to the right, to intercept a stone wall. Keep left along the wall descending to find, in a few hundred paces, a ladder stile leading over the wall into the upper woods of Rob Rash. A steep descent leads down to the road. Cross this directly, and go through the gap in the wall next to the large double gates. Descend a track to meet up with the outward route. Bear right to return to Elterwater village.

THE VALLEY BOTTOM

Easy tracks connect for a rare low-level glimpse
of some of Lakeland's most famous hills.

Great Langdale – the big, long valley – has always played a key role in the
story of the Lake District. In the 1920s there was a slightly unseemly row here,
between outdoor enthusiasts and conservationists. The former, led by T E
Leonard's Holiday Fellowship, wanted to build a campsite at the head of the
dale in Mickleden, closer to the fine crags and mountains that inspired them.
The latter, under the leadership of Dr G M Trevelyan opposed this intrusion
into a landscape barely touched by human intervention for 200 years.
The two men were pioneers of a new way of seeing the countryside, both
passionately committed to its recreational value to the common man – the
modern Youth Hostel Association is still headquartered in Trevelyan House.
After a few public letters, Leonard relented.

Perfect Stone

Five thousand years ago the valley would have looked very different, without
the farms and field boundaries established from medieval times. On the
high slopes of the Langdale Pikes however, the shapely crags that form the
valley's northern boundary, neolithic man had discovered the perfect stone
for shaping into axes. Axes made with Langdale's distinctive stone have been
unearthed from neolithic sites all over Britain and Ireland and even a few in
Europe. These were the tools that cut down the trees that allowed farmers to
farm, and settlements to grow. Stone, brought from the mountains to where
food could be grown, must have taken on an almost religious significance.
But it would be several thousand years after those first farmers cleared the
upper reaches of this valley before there was anything obvious for us to see.

Walking through the valley now it is the stone walls that most obviously
draw our attention. The valley floor is separated from the open fell by a 'ring
garth'. Perhaps 13th century in origin, it would have protected the open valley
fields from the beasts grazing on the upland 'waste'. Later field divisions
followed, as agricultural techniques improved and the current field pattern
would have been established pretty much as we see it today by the end of
the 18th century.

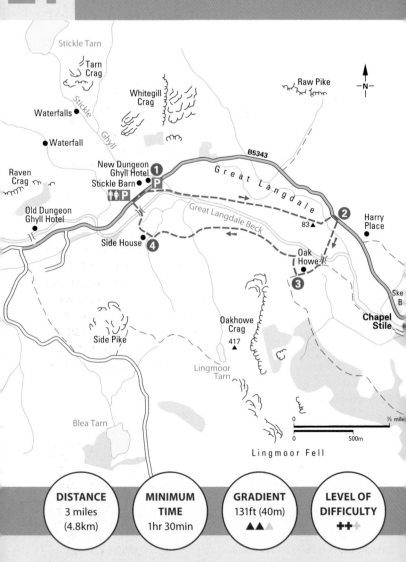

DISTANCE	MINIMUM TIME	GRADIENT	LEVEL OF DIFFICULTY
3 miles (4.8km)	1hr 30min	131ft (40m) ▲▲▲	✚✚✚

PATHS Stony tracks (some enclosed) and rocky paths **LANDSCAPE** Meadows and fell in valley bottom **SUGGESTED MAP** OS Explorers OL6 The English Lakes (SW) and OL7 The English Lakes (SE) **START/FINISH** Grid reference: NY295063 (on OL6) **DOG FRIENDLINESS** Some fields grazed by sheep, so take care towards Oak Howe **PARKING** Choice of National Trust or National Park Authority pay-and-display car parks at Stickle Ghyll near the head of Great Langdale **PUBLIC TOILETS** National Trust Stickle Ghyll car park

WALK 21 DIRECTIONS

❶ Locate a right of way at the back of the National Park Authority car park opposite the Stickle Barn. Follow this enclosed byway heading down the valley. In time the track meanders back across the valley side and up to the main road. Turn right here, with care and follow the road for 40yds (37m) to a bridleway turning on the right signposted to Base Brown.

❷ A pair of gates leads out on to the virtually flat valley bottom. A gated bridge takes you over Langdale Beck and on the far side turn right up a farm track heading for a white farm building at Oak Howe.

❸ Beyond the buildings turn right at a signpost on an enclosed footpath skirting the flank of the little hill and descending to a gate. Beyond this a muddy track follows the base of the open fell with a wall on the right. The path ascends gradually and is a little rough underfoot in places. The ascent continues to a high point beyond a single slate bridge, the walls converging to a gate. Beyond this it descends briskly towards buildings at Side House.

> **🦋 ON THE WALK**
> You'll see a number of isolated ash and elm trees, their growth stunted by pollarding at some time in the past. This wasn't done for ornament, but to create a reliable supply of foliage. The leaves were fed to sheep, overwintering in the meadowlands of the valley bottom.

❹ Through a gate continue on a level path, cross a bridge and pass through a kissing gate into the farmyard. Bear right along the access track though another gate and beyond to a bridge over the Langdale Beck. Continue, emerging on the main valley road opposite the National Trust's Stickle Ghyll car park, turning right if you left your vehicle in the National Park Authority car park.

> **🍴 EATING AND DRINKING**
> The Stickle Barn, a pub at the top of the National Trust car park at the start, is the nearest and caters for most tastes. There's a huge open air seating area out front, perfect for watching the sun go down over the surrounding fells. Near by the Old and New Dungeon Ghyll hotels also offer good food and beer.

> **🌀 IN THE AREA**
> Carry on the minor road at the head of the valley and pass over the col into Little Langdale. First you'll see Blea Tarn, sheltering beneath the watchful crags of Side Pike, then you'll come to the main valley with its tarn and pub. At Fell Foot, the Ting Mound may be where Norse settlers made their parliament in the 9th century.

BOOT AND THE NARROW-GAUGE TRACK

Explore the heart of lovely Eskdale and discover its diminutive railway past.

The Ravenglass and Eskdale Railway , 'La'al Ratty', opened in 1875, from the main line railway at Ravenglass to Boot. Though ostensibly to serve the copper mines at Nab Gill, it carried passengers also and a poster of 1884 advertised four trains a day (no Sunday service) to 'The foot of Scawfell in the English Alps'.

The line's original gauge was 3ft (914mm) and the station at Boot was right up against the foot of the fell, beyond the village mill and the packhorse bridge over the Whillan Beck. Contemporary photographs depict crowds of tourists thronging along the single platform, disembarking from packed wagons. But tourists were not enough to keep the line alive, and as the mines faltered, so did Ratty. In April 1913 both mines and railway closed, and this time it felt like the end.

Model Railway Enthusiasts

But as the nation struggled through the dark days of World War I, a peculiar thing happened. A pair of model railway enthusiasts, W J Bassett-Lowke and R Proctor-Mitchell, bought the whole line and set about relaying the track to suit their tiny engines. By 1916, this new 15-in (381mm) gauge track covered its full length, and once more trains were running. The scaled-down locomotives found the incline up to Nab Gill at Boot too severe however, and soon trains were terminating around Dalegarth, where in 1880 an extension had been constructed to serve mines at Gill Force on the opposite side of the valley. Building a new station by the main valley road, with a turntable so the engines could always operate running forwards 'La'al Ratty' was reborn and has been running ever since. Industry returned to the line when the granite quarry at Beckfoot was opened up, and for a period the twin revenues of tourists and crushed stone seemed enough to keep it open. But by 1960 money once again became short. This time a group of volunteers stepped in, backed by Sir Wavell Wakefield. The formula clearly worked, as by 2007 pop pioneer and railway enthusiast Pete Waterman was able to offer his celebrity endorsement to a brand new station complex at Dalegarth, with a much improved visitor centre and restaurant.

Opposite: Eskdale at dawn above Boot

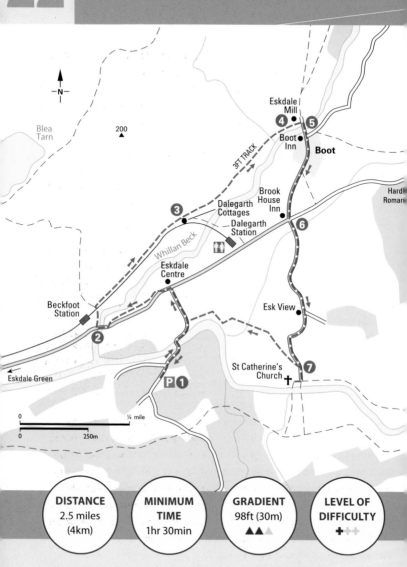

DISTANCE	MINIMUM TIME	GRADIENT	LEVEL OF DIFFICULTY
2.5 miles (4km)	1hr 30min	98ft (30m) ▲▲▲	+++

PATHS Roads, grassy paths and tracks, 3 stiles **LANDSCAPE** Woods, fields, fell, and valley **SUGGESTED MAP** OS Explorer OL6 The English Lakes (SW) **START/FINISH** Grid reference: NY 170001 **DOG FRIENDLINESS** Take care on road sections and where sheep graze beyond Dalegarth Cottages **PARKING** Trough House car park, off main valley road opposite Eskdale Centre between Dalegarth and Beckfoot stations **PUBLIC TOILETS** At Dalegarth Station

WALK 22 DIRECTIONS

❶ Walk back on to the road and turn right, following it over Trough House Bridge and on past the war memorial to a T-junction in front of the Eskdale Centre (formerly a school). Turn left along the road for a few paces, past the entrance to the vicarage before dipping in to the woods on the right. On the far side of this little parking area you'll find a narrow track between the road and the Whillan Beck offers a pleasant alternative to walking along the main valley road (although this isn't very busy). Soon you have to emerge again on the road for a few more paces to cross the bridge over Whillan Beck.

❷ Continue on the right-hand side to the access road on the right and turn up past the tiny platform of Beckfoot Station. Cross the railway line with care and continue on the lineside track into the woods. Soon the line sweeps off to the right, in front of Dalegarth Cottages, but you stay on the left hand route, around the back of the cottages.

❸ Cross a stile and you will see another sign for the '3ft Track'. Continue along the obvious former trackbed at the foot of the fell. Cross two more stiles and approach the old terminus beyond a tumbledown farm building.

❹ Walk up the former terminus platform and at the far end pass the ruined terminus buildings. Beyond this follow the track alongside a wall on your right to a gate. Go though this and descend into Boot Main Street, crossing a packhorse bridge and passing the old watermill on your left.

❺ Continue down the street past the shop and the Boot Inn, to the T-junction with the main valley road by the Brook House Inn.

> ### ⌀ IN THE AREA
> Why not brave the terrifying road bends at the top of the valley and explore the fantastic remains of Hardknott Roman fort. Known to the soldiers as *Mediobogdum*, it must have felt a long way from the Adriatic. The view into upper Eskdale from the far side is particularly impressive.

❻ Cross the road and follow the track opposite, jinking right past the buildings of Esk View. Continue to a junction on the right. You can carry on to visit St Catherine's Church here with its idyllic riverside setting, then return to this spot to follow the enclosed footpath.

❼ Stay on the path through a gate and eventually up a bank to another gate out on to a minor road. Turn left here to return to to Trough House Bridge. Just over the bridge, turn left through a gap in the wall and cross a woody bluff to emerge at the back of the car park.

THE
ROMAN PORT

Discover the surprising Roman legacy in the Lake District National Park's only seaport.

Ravenglass doesn't feel like a thriving port. Its single main street ends at an ominous looking floodgate, and the pretty houses have names like the Old Bakery, the Old Reading Room and the Old Butchers. The last tall-masted cargo ship sailed into the bay in 1914, and most visitors who come here, perhaps on 'La'al Ratty' from Eskdale seem surprised to see the sea at all. The Lake District isn't really about coast after all.

The Romans

But wind back the clock nearly 2,000 years and things are very different. In AD 78 or 79 General Julius Agricola was here contemplating the next steps in his Imperial conquest of the islands. Here on the tidal river bank, he built a hasty fort of earth and timber, leaving its day-to-day control to a garrison of Germans. *Glannoventa* – 'the town on the river bank' grew in stature. As Hadrian asserted his control on Rome's northern frontier 50 years later, the fort was expanded to an impressive 3.6 acres (1.5ha) and formed the last outward face of a vast new barrier, which stretched all the way to the east coast at Tynemouth. Inland, the Roman road named the 10th *iter* ran up Eskdale to the eyrie-like garrison fort at Hardknott, then over the fells to Ambleside, Kendal and the main roads to the south.

Bath House

By AD 300 there was an extensive town in the lee of the fort and, at its eastern corner, it boasted a state of the art bath house, complete with hypocaust underfloor heating. What's really remarkable, though about *Glannoventa's* bath house, is that 1,700 years later, it's still there, in a corner of woodland, by a farm track near the railway line. Shown on modern maps as Walls Castle, the impressive remnants stand up to 12ft (3.7m) high and even bear traces of their original plaster. A niche stands out on one wall, where once a statue of the emperor or the goddess Fortuna would have watched over the bathers.

Of the fort itself there is little to see. Over 90ft (27m) has been lost to the ever-changing course of the estuary and the sea.

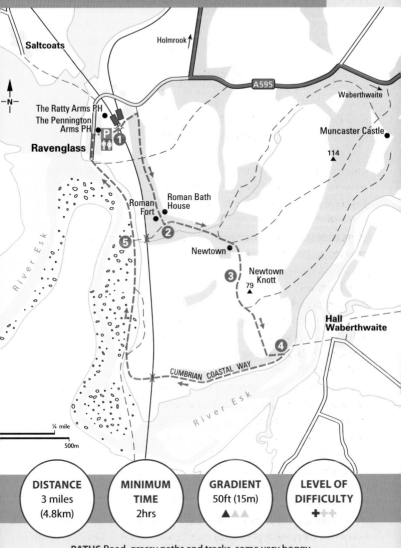

Saltcoats
Holmrook↑
A595
Waberthwaite
The Ratty Arms PH
The Pennington
Arms PH
Muncaster Castle
P
114
Ravenglass
Roman Bath
House
Roman
Fort
Newtown
Newtown
Knott
79
Hall
Waberthwaite
CUMBRIAN COASTAL WAY
River Esk
River Esk
¼ mile
500m

DISTANCE	MINIMUM TIME	GRADIENT	LEVEL OF DIFFICULTY
3 miles (4.8km)	2hrs	50ft (15m) ▲▲▲	✚✚✚

PATHS Road, grassy paths and tracks, some very boggy
LANDSCAPE Tidal marsh, foreshore woods and fields
SUGGESTED MAP OS Explorer OL6 The English Lakes (SW) **START/FINISH** Grid reference: SD 085964 **DOG FRIENDLINESS** One field grazed by sheep, otherwise suitable for dogs **PARKING** Ravenglass village car park
PUBLIC TOILETS At car park **NOTE** The foreshore section of this walk may be impassable for up to 2 hours either side of high tides more than 23ft 7in (7.2m) at Barrow. Check tide times locally or on the BBC Cumbria website

WALK 23 DIRECTIONS

1 Leave the car park by the top-right corner, signposted 'Roman Bath House'. Cross the railway bridge and pass the station complex and children's play area on the left, following the snicketway beyond to a gate. Through this turn immediately right along a lane. Soon pick up a path on the left running parallel with the road, waymarked 'Muncaster'.

2 Shortly arrive at the Roman Bath House. Very little is visible of the Roman fort. Continue beyond the Bath House, keeping left at a junction with the signs for Muncaster. Stay on the main track as it winds round towards the farm buildings at Newtown. Ignore signs off to the left, but continue round the back of the farm buildings and on through a gate to a gateway in the boundary wall of the castle park.

3 Bear right through this along a muddy track, keeping the wall on your right as you skirt round the foot of Newtown Knott. (Newtown Knott is open access land so you can scramble to its summit if you have the time). On the far side of the Knott, keep right, descending to a large gate in the wall. Walk down the field heading for a kissing gate at the bottom beyond a clump of gorse. Through this continue into the woods to a junction. Turn left and in a few paces turn right, by a Cumbria Coastal Way sign, which should have a current tide timetable.

4 Observe the warning notices about high tides here and if it is safe to proceed walk out through the gateway on to the marshy foreshore of the Esk estuary. Turn right and follow the marshside path as it winds in and out of rushes and over little streams, finally straightening to pass under a railway bridge. On the other side continue round the corner, with the estuary now deepening and the spit of land supporting the Eskmeals dunes narrowing your horizon. Stay at the head of the beach passing another railway bridge and ignoring the track that goes through it.

> ### 🍴 EATING AND DRINKING
> The Pennington Arms in Ravenglass has been made over in recent years and now boasts a boutiquy feel, though its still a nice place to drop in for a stylish bite to eat. More robust fayre, and probably a warmer welcome for pooch, can be found at the Ratty Arms by the station.

5 Just beyond, climb a flight of steps up the bank to a level, grassy area, where some benches boast fine views across the estuary and dunes to the open sea beyond. The grassy path descends back to shore level. Now follow the track in front of the houses to reach the floodgate at the bottom of Ravenglass's main street. Turn right here and walk up the street, turning right at the Pennington Arms to return to the car park.

BRITAIN'S FAVOURITE VIEW

Lakeside and woodland paths lead to Britain's favourite view.

Voted 'Britain's favourite view' in 2007, Wastwater is still a remote spot. Despite its credentials as England's deepest lake (258ft/79m), overlooked by its highest hill, Scafell Pike (3208ft/978m), Wastwater is still hard to reach from the Lake District's honeypots by any other means than walking over Sty Head or Black Sail. It's well over an hour by car from Windermere and that's barely 30 miles (48km) away.

Cosmopolitan Place

Wasdale wasn't always this remote. In the days when a sailing ship was the fastest means of getting anywhere, the dale's position, opening out on to the fertile coastal plain of West Cumbria, was really quite beneficial. The lower valley, beyond the lake, is known as Nether Wasdale. Many farms here prospered in the 18th century in a way unimagined by those deeper into the fells. They had threshing machines and grew turnips and pedigree pigs when the fell sheep farmers were still using methods unchanged since the time they were run by great medieval monasteries. Slate, copper and wool from the Lakeland fells all passed this way on horseback, on the way to the bustling new port at Whitehaven. In the opposite direction went ginger and cinnamon, sugar and tobacco from the West Indies.

It's hard to imagine, but this must have been a relatively cosmopolitan place. In 1832 Rawson Stansfield, a wealthy banker from Halifax bought land at Daker End and Low Wood, by the mouth of Wastwater. By 1839 he had settled in his newly built mock-Tudor style Wasdale Hall and set about the valley doing good works.

But so far from the booming tourist crowds, little else changed in this quiet backwater. The National Trust secured Wasdale Hall and Low Wood in 1959, finally giving the rest of us access to *that* view from its best vantage point. The Hall is now a youth hostel, but electricity didn't arrive in the upper valley until 1978, so the pace of life has not really quickened. Ironically for the valley, many who pass this way today do so in the middle of the night, on their way to rush up Scafell Pike as a second leg in a Three Peaks challenge.

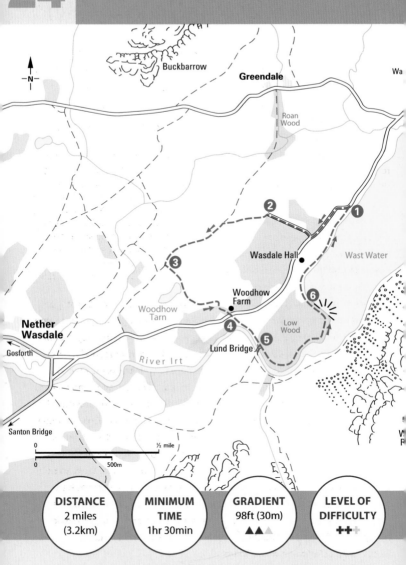

DISTANCE
2 miles
(3.2km)

**MINIMUM
TIME**
1hr 30min

GRADIENT
98ft (30m)
▲▲▲

**LEVEL OF
DIFFICULTY**
✦✦✦

PATHS Road, grassy paths and tracks, 2 stiles **LANDSCAPE** Woods, fields
and lakeside **SUGGESTED MAP** OS Explorer OL6 The English Lakes (SW)
START/FINISH Grid reference: NY 148048
DOG FRIENDLINESS Fields grazed by sheep, but after Lund Bridge
you should be fine **PARKING** Roadside parking by the lake between the
Greendale turn and a cattle grid **PUBLIC TOILETS** None on route, nearest in
Wasdale Head (3 miles/4.8km)

WALK 24 DIRECTIONS

❶ From your parking area, walk west along the lake road, heading for a cattle grid at a bend. Continue with care for about 200yds (183m) and take a footpath signed up to the right. A broad track leads up amid woods. The remains of a walled garden appear on the right and beyond this the track becomes a little rougher.

❷ At a ladder stile you emerge from the walled path to bear left with a grassy path across more open country. Meandering through the bog cotton and over a little bridge, you soon pick up a more substantial bridleway coming in from Greendale. This wider track continues across the access land at Ashness How descending to a gate and stile beneath a gentle ramp of crag. Beyond this, continue to a footpath sign beside a fallen tree.

❸ Turn left, with the direction for Woodhow and pass though a gate. The path swings round to the right passing the secretive waters of Woodhow Tarn (not accessible). At the next gate bear left up the track towards Woodhow Farm. Approaching the farm, heed the diversion signs that take you over an adjacent bluff and deliver you at the farm gate, back on the road.

❹ Cross and turn left for a few paces to a footpath sign and gate on the right. Go through this and down the field beyond, descending to the River Irt and a gate leading onto a riverside path. Stay on this path as it enters Low Wood and reaches the Lund Bridge.

🍴 EATING AND DRINKING

You're spoiled for choice in Wasdale, though there isn't anywhere on the route. At the head of the valley the Wasdale Head Inn is legendary, serving robust food and real ale. Down the dale at Nether Wasdale, you'll find the Screes and the Strands pubs, either side of the village green and both offering decent food and good beer.

---

❺ Don't cross the bridge, but stay by the riverside, going through the kissing gate and into the woods. Stay with the lower path and as you round the bend you'll see a weir across the river. The water now becomes calmer and begins to open out into the lake, and there is a barn on the opposite bank. Continue round a little headland and beyond a boathouse you'll find yourself on the lakeshore proper. A terraced track skirts the shore and woods with the best views up the valley. Through a gate you enter the parkland around Wasdale Hall (now a youth hostel).

❻ Several more gates follow and you dive back into the rhododendrons opposite a little island and take a short flight of rocky steps leading upto a ladder stile. Turn left, and the road is just a few paces further on. Turn right to return to the parking areas by the shore.

WYTHBURN AND HARROP TARN

A steep climb up into a wooded hollow reveals a tarn
and a glimpse of a lost world.

Before 1875, the reservoir we now describe as Thirlmere was two natural glacial lakes – Leathes Water and Wythburn Water – connected by a narrow strip of slow moving beck, and ponderously crossed by a structure known as the Celtic Bridge. At Steel End, the hamlet of Wythburn was a ragtag of farms scattered across the valley head, from the old church on the fellside in the east, to the venerable farmhouse known as Westhead below Birk Crag in the west. In the valley bottom a collection of cottages went by the ironic name The City. There were two pubs, the Cherry Tree and the Nag's Head, which vied for the business of travellers passing over Dunmail Raise from west Cumbria towards Kendal. This was sheep farming territory, not unlike Langdale or Borrowdale; the tree cover that existed was mostly oak or ash, in small coppice woods or on rough land where even sheep couldn't penetrate.

Ambitious Plan

But that all changed, because faraway Manchester, the first metropolis of the industrial age, was running out of water. Cotton goods from the world's cotton capital were being shipped to Glasgow for bleaching and dyeing, because the water that Manchester was wringing from the adjacent south Pennines was too peat stained to be of use. The Waterworks Committee, under the guidance of its formidable chairman Sir John Harwood, set about an ambitious plan to take the sparkling clean water from the Wyth Burn to the taps of Cheetham Hill.

Cutting through opposition with dogged determination, the land was bought, and by 1894 a dam was built and the valley was flooded. Farms not actually inundated, were soon abandoned – you pass Stenkin's barns and Westhead's sad ruins, still with cobbles in the yard and traces of plaster on the tumbled walls. Trees were planted to stabilise the fellsides – Norway and Sitka spruce, larch and Douglas fir, previously unseen in plantations in England. A new road was built down the west of the valley, and much later car parks and walking trails to add a new 'amenity' value. It's still a beautiful place, but that current beauty is a relatively recent creation.

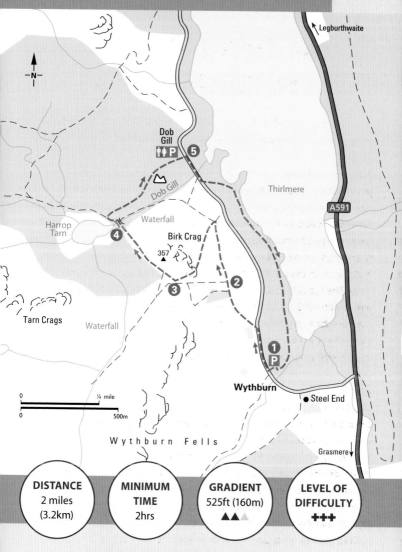

↑ Legburthwaite

Dob Gill
🚻 P ❺

Thirlmere

A591

Dob Gill

Waterfall

Harrop
Tarn

❹

Birk Crag

357 ▲

❸   ❷

Tarn Crags

Waterfall

❶
P

Wythburn   • Steel End

W y t h b u r n   F e l l s

0 ____ ¼ mile
0 _____ 500m

Grasmere ↓

—N—

DISTANCE
2 miles
(3.2km)

**MINIMUM
TIME**
2hrs

GRADIENT
525ft (160m)
▲▲▲

**LEVEL OF
DIFFICULTY**
+++

PATHS Road, rough fell track and nature trail
LANDSCAPE Fell, forest and lakeside
SUGGESTED MAP OS Explorer OL5 The English Lakes (NE)
START/FINISH Grid reference: NY 320130
DOG FRIENDLINESS Sheep in the fields at the start and not much subsequent
scope for wandering off **PARKING** Steel End pay-and-display car park
PUBLIC TOILETS At Dob Gill car park

WALK 25 DIRECTIONS

❶ Leave the parking area by the main entrance and turn right along the minor road for 200yds (183m). At a footpath sign on the left by some buildings, turn left and walk through the yard, passing through several gates to enter a field. Keep to the base of the field by the wall, ascending gently to the remains of West End farmhouse.

❷ Continue through the ruins, through a gate, then a small field. Another gate leads you through to a boggy area, the path dipping towards a final gate. Don't go through this, but turn left, on a faint rising path zig-zagging back steeply up the hill. Across a tongue of drier land, you are now heading for the gap between two sets of crags on the horizon. As you get closer to the crag, you'll find a shelving path heading up to the left. A series of underused rocky steps lead you up into the gap between the crags and a shallow col, the slopes now cloaked in juniper. At the top of the crag, the path reaches a dry-stone wall running up the fell.

❸ Follow this over the brow ahead. Levelling out now, you'll see the forest beyond, a viewpoint on Birk Crag up to the left making for a worthy diversion. At the wall junction, step through a gap, into a boggy channel which becomes a path between the wall and the forest fence. An obvious route now recrosses the wall and descends with the wall on your left into the valley of

🍴 EATING AND DRINKING

Nothing remains of the Cherry Tree or the Nag's Head at Wythburn but further down the valley you can still find the King's Head at Thirlspot, serving good food, as it did long before the arrival of the reservoir.

Harrop Tarn. At the bottom of the slope a boardwalk leads to a gate in the deer fence. Turn right and follow the forest trail to a bridge over the tarn's outflow.

❹ Cross the bridge and follow the prominent tarnside track round a corner. After a few paces, turn right with a trail marker, over a low bluff then joining a paved pathway down the left-hand side of the descending gill. Soon the roar of a waterfall on your right alerts you to some unprotected viewpoints. Green and yellow waymarkers abound as the descent becomes steeper, zig-zagging down into older woodlands. A line of blue-topped posts marks your steep route, which soon becomes more gentle, beneath beeches to a gate at the junction of a wall and fence. Walk out into Dob Gill car park (toilets).

❺ Turn right along the road, recrossing Dob Gill and spotting a turn on the left marked 'lakeshore path'. Go through the kissing gate and follow the lakeshore path back to Steel End car park. When the water level is very high, this route can be flooded. In this case, walk back to Steel End along the road.

ALONG ULLSWATER'S SHORE TO SILVER POINT

From the shores of Ullswater to one
of its most spectacular viewpoints.

The elongated hamlet of Patterdale has a rugged, mountain quality. Sited below the mighty Helvellyn massif its straggle of houses, inn, hotel, mountain rescue base, church and school have a bleakness about them. A perfect contrast to the splendour of Ullswater, whose southern shore lies hardly a stone's throw away. This walk strolls through mixed woodland and open aspect above the shores of the lake to visit the famed viewpoint of Silver Point. The adventurous may wish to make the scramble to the top of Silver Crag, as did horsedrawn coach parties of old, for a better view of the lake.

Ullswater

Undoubtedly one of the loveliest of the lakes, the three legs of Ullswater add up to a total length of 7.5 miles (12.1km) with an average width of 0.5 mile (800m) and a maximum depth of 205ft (62.5m). It is Lakeland's second largest lake, not quite measuring up to Windermere. Its waters are exceptionally clear and in the deepest part of the lake, off Howtown, lives a curious fish called the schelly; a creature akin to a freshwater herring.

Apart from rescue and Park Ranger launches, you won't see many power boats here, but Ullswater 'Steamers' have three boats operating between Glenridding and Pooley Bridge during the summer. Alfred Wainwright (1907–91), known for his seven *Pictorial Guides to the Lakeland Fells*, regarded this to be a part of one of the most beautiful walks in the Lakes. Preservation of the lake in its present form is due to a concerted campaign, led in Parliament by Lord Birkett, against the proposed Manchester Corporation Water Act in 1965. Although the act was passed, and water is extracted from the lake, the workings are hidden underground and designed in such a way as to make it impossible to lower the water level beyond the agreed limit.

Among the trees, beside the shore, it was the golden yellow daffodils of this lake that inspired William Wordsworth's most widely known poem, 'I wandered lonely as a cloud' or 'Daffodils' as it often referred to (published in 1807). His sister Dorothy recorded the event vividly in her diary and there is no doubt that this later helped William to pen his famous verse.

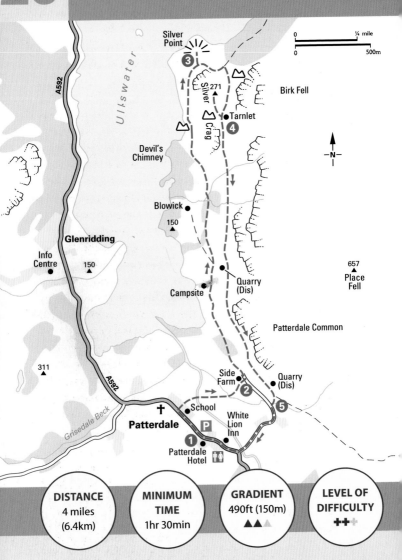

DISTANCE
4 miles
(6.4km)

MINIMUM
TIME
1hr 30min

GRADIENT
490ft (150m)
▲▲△

LEVEL OF
DIFFICULTY
++✛

PATHS Stony tracks and paths, no stiles **LANDSCAPE** Lake and fell views, mixed
woodland **SUGGESTED MAP** OS Explorer OL5 The English Lakes (NE)
START/FINISH Grid reference: NY 396159
DOG FRIENDLINESS Passes through working farm and open hillside grazed
by sheep, dogs must be under control at all times
PARKING Pay-and-display car park opposite Patterdale Hotel
PUBLIC TOILETS Opposite White Lion in Patterdale village centre

WALK 26 DIRECTIONS

1 From the car park walk to the road and turn right towards the shore of Ullswater. Pass the school to follow a track leading off right, through the buildings. Follow the unsurfaced track over a bridge and continue through the buildings of Side Farm to join another unsurfaced track.

2 Turn left along the undulating track, with a stone wall to the left, and pass through mixed woodland, predominantly oak and ash, before open fellside appears above. Proceed along the path above the campsite and pass a stand of larch before descending to cross a little stream above the buildings of Blowick, seen through the trees below. The path ascends again to crest a craggy knoll above the woods of Devil's Chimney. Make a steep descent following the path through the rocks before it levels to traverse beneath the craggy heights of Silver Crag. A slight ascent, passing some fine holly trees, gains the shoulder of Silver Point and an outstanding view of Ullswater. A short there-and-back to the tip is worthwhile.

3 Follow the path, which sweeps beneath the end of Silver Crag and continue to pass a small stream before a steep stony path, eroded in places, breaks off to the right. Ascend this, climbing diagonally right, through the juniper bushes. Gain the narrow gap which separates Silver Crag to the right from the main hillside of Birk Fell to the left. This little valley is quite boggy and holds a small tarnlet.

4 If you don't care for steep, exposed ground, follow the high narrow path to make a gradual descent south in the direction of Patterdale. But for those with a head for heights, a short steep scramble leads to the top of Silver Crag and a wonderful view. Care must be exercised for steep ground lies in all directions. Descend back to the ravine and the main path by the same route. The path is easy though it traverses the open fellside and may be boggy in places. Pass open quarry workings, where there is a large unfenced hole next to the path (take care), and continue on, to cross over the slate scree of a larger quarry. Bear right to descend by a stream and cross a little footbridge leading to the gate at the end of a track.

🍴 **EATING AND DRINKING**

On the route, Side Farm sometimes offers teas and ice creams and, in the centre of Patterdale, next to the road, stands the White Lion Inn which serves bar meals throughout the year.

---

5 Go left through the gate and then follow the lane which leads through the meadows. Cross the bridge and join the road. Bear right through Patterdale to return to the car park and the start of the walk.

ACROSS HEUGHSCAR HILL'S ROMAN ROAD

This walk leads to views over the second largest lake in the region, crosses a Roman road and takes in artefacts of prehistory.

This is a relatively gentle and straightforward hill walk, traversing green turf, bracken and white limestone pavement. It offers extensive views west over Ullswater, north across the stone buildings of Pooley Bridge and east to the agricultural plains of the Eden Valley. Features of the walk include crossing the High Street Roman road and an examination of the fascinating remains from prehistory found on Moor Divock.

Antiquities of Moor Divock

Ancient relics of prehistory, scattered across the high shoulder of Moor Divock, add an air of mystery and intrigue to this outing. The short section of the High Street Roman road taken on this walk leads to the distinct and unmistakeable Cockpit stone circle. Two concentric stone circles, some standing, some fallen, contain a stone and earth circular bank up to 3ft (1m) high. It has an internal radius of around 85ft (26m) and, as it is thought to be of Bronze Age origin, *c*2000 BC, it predates the Roman road. In more recent times, it was most probably used for cockfighting. This pastime, once popular in the Lake District, was outlawed in 1849.

Crouched Skeleton

Extending south-east from here is desolate Moor Divock where, hidden among the stark landscape of coarse hill grass, bracken, heather and bog, are many prehistoric burial mounds and cairns. A mound known as White Raise, presumably because of the white quartz that marks its rocks, when partially excavated in the 19th century revealed a crouched skeleton in one of its cists (a coffin or burial chamber of stone or wood). Near by, the Cop Stone, a knarled standing stone some 5ft (1.5m) high, tops a low hill and provides a direction indicator in this otherwise rather featureless landscape. Local sports were held by this stone up until 1800 and tradition claims that an avenue of standing stones known as the Shap Avenue once led to it. Near by, two further Bronze Age stone circles referred to as Moor Divock 4 and Moor Divock 5, have been partially excavated to reveal urns and ashes.

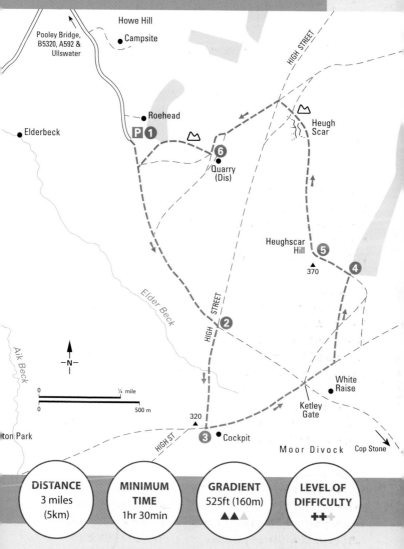

Howe Hill

• Campsite

• Roehead

P **1**

• Elderbeck

6

Quarry (Dis)

HIGH STREET

Heugh Scar

Heughscar Hill

5

▲ 370

4

Elder Beck

HIGH STREET

Aik Beck

—N—

0 ¼ mile

0 500 m

2

White Raise •

Ketley Gate

320 ▲

HIGH ST

3 • Cockpit

Moor Divock

Cop Stone

ton Park

DISTANCE	MINIMUM TIME	GRADIENT	LEVEL OF DIFFICULTY
3 miles (5km)	1hr 30min	525ft (160m) ▲▲▲	++✛

PATHS Stony tracks, grassy tracks and hillside **LANDSCAPE** Mostly open fell
SUGGESTED MAP OS Explorer OL5 The English Lakes (NE)
START/FINISH Grid reference: NY 478235
DOG FRIENDLINESS Under strict control as sheep and ponies roam open fell
PARKING Roadside parking at Roehead, on minor road above Pooley Bridge. Do not block any driveways. If the parking area is full, the only alternative is to park in Pooley Bridge and walk up the road **PUBLIC TOILETS** Pooley Bridge village centre

WALK 27 DIRECTIONS

1 At Roehead the road end is indicated by a pair of gates leading onto the moor. Go through the gates and climb the wide track, continuing to where the going levels and the track crosses another one, coming down from the south-west, by a low cairn. This is the High Street Roman road.

2 Bear right along the prominent line of the Roman road to reach a low circular ancient wall of earth and stone. This, the Cockpit, is the largest of the prehistoric antiquities on Moor Divock.

🍴 EATING AND DRINKING

There are numerous cafés and inns in Pooley Bridge. Particularly notable is the Sun, an unspoiled 18th-century coaching inn. It offers excellent bar meals and a fine range of real ales brewed at the local Jennings Brewery in Cockermouth.

---

3 A way leads back diagonally north by the shallow shake holes (sinkholes) to the original track at Ketley Gate. A little to the right, the White Raise burial cairn is worthy of attention. Go straight ahead here, following the track which leads north-east, ascending towards a walled wood high on the hillside. Turn left with an upward crossing path, which leads to the wall corner.

4 Bear left along the ridge, before heading off right to find the top of Heughscar Hill. The flat summit of the hill occupies a commanding position offering rewarding views.

5 Proceed north along the high shoulder to pass the broken little limestone crag of Heugh Scar below to the left. At the end of the scar make a steep descent of the grassy hillside, crossing a track and continuing down to the point where another track and the grassy lane of the High Street Roman road cross each other. Descend to the left, taking the track that passes below the Roman road and head in the general direction of Ullswater.

6 Continue the descent to the corner of a stone wall marked by a large sycamore tree. Follow the route that falls steeply down beside the wall. Bear left near the bottom of the incline and gain the original broad track just above the gates near Roehead.

🌿 IN THE AREA

Just beyond Pooley Bridge, the shores of Ullswater, the region's second largest lake some 7.5 miles (12.1km) long, are a fine place to contemplate the beauty of the Lake District. Two beautifully preserved 19th-century boats, *Lady of the Lake* and *Raven*, run regular trips from the jetty stopping at the landing stages at Howtown and Glenridding.

GOWBARROW FELL AND AIRA FORCE

To the summit of a fell famous for its beauty, returning through a waterfall-filled gorge.

Gowbarrow (it's pronounced 'Gowbro') Fell rises above Ullswater's northern shore, the first arm of the hill country that leads eventually to Helvellyn's lofty summit. A deer park from medieval times, along with nearby Glencoyne, it would have once been stocked with fallow deer to tempt aristocratic sportsmen. In the 1780s the Howards of Greystoke transformed an old rustic barn into the fancifully named Lyulph's Tower and claimed to trace their lineage to some ancient ruler of the region, so it was already a known beauty spot when the Wordsworth's rambled past in 1802, on their way home to Grasmere from Thomas Clarkson's house at Eusemere near Pooley Bridge. Dorothy's description in her diary of the journey is wonderfully prosaic. 'When we were in the woods beyond Gowbarrow Park we saw a few daffodils close to the water'. Her brother turned the experience into perhaps his most famous lines in 'Daffodils' in 1804:

> 'When all at once I saw a crowd,
> A host of golden daffodils.'

Pleasure Garden

The Howards kept developing their lakeside estate, creating a pleasure garden from the tumbling Aira Beck with its magnificent falls. Bridges and pathways were followed by a full-blown arboretum of Sitka spruce, cedars and Douglas firs, many of which you can still see today. But the onset of the 20th century saw more pressing calls on their cash and in 1906 the Gowbarrow Estate was divided into building plots and put up for sale. A public hue and cry followed, engineered by the formidable pairing of Octavia Hill and Canon Rawnsley. Over £12,000 was raised by public subscription and de Quincy's 'most romantic of parks' was saved for posterity by the National Trust. The opening ceremony was attended by one Woodrow Wilson, whose mother came from Carlisle and who was yet to become the 28th President of the United States. The National Trust still owns the land and much more around Ullswater, having ensured that it was to become a place of beauty to be enjoyed by the many, not the privileged few.

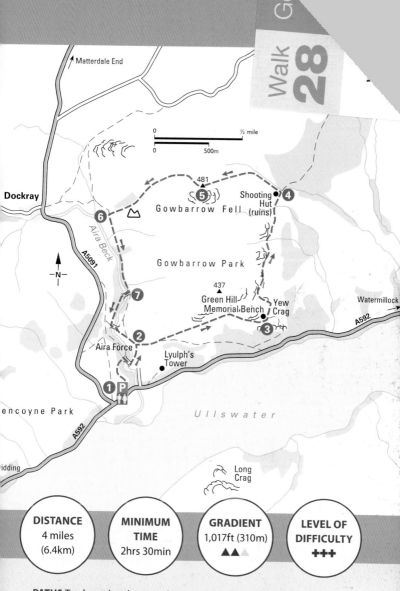

Matterdale End

Dockray

481 ▲
⑤

Shooting
Hut
(ruins) ④

Gowbarrow Fell

⑥

Aira Beck

A5091

Gowbarrow Park

437 ▲
Green Hill
Memorial Bench

Yew
Crag

Watermillock

A592

⑦

③

②

Aira Force

Lyulph's
Tower

① P

encoyne Park

A592

U l l s w a t e r

idding

Long
Crag

–N–

0 .... ½ mile
0 .... 500m

DISTANCE
4 miles
(6.4km)

**MINIMUM
TIME**
2hrs 30min

GRADIENT
1,017ft (310m)
▲▲▲

**LEVEL OF
DIFFICULTY**
+++

PATHS Tracks and paths, some boggy, some quite rocky and steep; 1 stile
LANDSCAPE Fells, riverside gorge and lake
SUGGESTED MAP OS Explorer OL5 The English Lakes (NE)
START/FINISH Grid reference: NY 400200
DOG FRIENDLINESS Fells grazed by sheep, so should be under close control
for the first couple of miles **PARKING** National Trust pay-and-display car park
at Aira Force off the A592 **PUBLIC TOILETS** At car park

Opposite: View over Ullswater from Gowbarrow Fell

WALK 28 DIRECTIONS

❶ Walk through the gateway at the top of the car park, and then a gate following a path into the trees. Keep right, descending steps to a bridge. Cross the bridge and walk up the steps beyond. At the top, fork right up another short flight to join a path close to a boundary fence. After 120yds (110m) go through a gate in the fence on the right and walk out onto the fell.

❷ Now follow a rising grassy path as it rakes up the fellside. Keep to the right-hand path initially then at a junction take the left-hand path rising up the fell. Follow this route, eventually rounding a corner by a memorial bench, where you'll see a viewpoint, accessed by a stile on the right.

❸ Returning to the main path continue as it cuts into the crags on a rocky shelf, before descending towards a wall and gate. Don't go through the gate but turn left a few paces before it by the ruins of an old shooting hut.

❹ A narrower path now rises up a little valley and across a stream and bogs. Swinging left up the hill as you approach a crossing wall, the route has been engineered to cross the bogs and your direction of travel is obvious.

❺ Turn left at a T-junction with a made track, visit the summit, before returning to the junction and this time keeping ahead on the made path until it peters out. Stay with this direction heading for a wall, then bear left beside it, steepening in a series of zig-zags. Passing to the left of a plantation the steep path finally reaches a ladder stile into a boggy field. Across this a path line can be identified, meeting a substantial track at a T-junction.

🍴 EATING AND DRINKING

There's a café by the National Trust car park, serving teas and coffees, light lunches and snacks. If you're after something more substantial try the Royal Hotel at Dockray.

---

❻ Turn left here to a gate into woodland. Now follow the obvious descending track, never straying far from the beck on your right. Through a gap in a wall there are plenty of viewing points, but where the path forks the lower option takes you down to a bridge above the falls. Cross this and continue downstream now on the opposite bank. Rounding a corner as the water cascades into a deep chasm, pass through a gate and turn left down steps to a bridge. Cross it and turn right down a steep flight of stone steps.

❼ Turn right for another view of the gorge, then return to this point and carry on down the terraced path above the gill. Eventually your downward route meets your outward route. Cross the bridge on the right and walk up the far side, turning left in the little enclosure to return to the car park.

ACROSS THE MOSSES OF THE CALDEW

Quiet lanes and farm tracks lead across the marshlands that line the River Caldew, in the shadow of Carrock Fell.

This is a boundary walk, in more ways than one. Driving towards the Lake District on the A66 from Penrith, you'll barely notice the rise of the limestone uplands that form their white stone 'polo mint' around the core of the Lakeland fells. But as you enter the National Park, and drop down the bank from the junction at Troutbeck, something changes. Ahead of you the massif of Skiddaw and Blencathra rears up like an alpine vision – all pointy summits and airy ridges. As with many geographical features, there's a bit of geology going on here, followed by a healthy dose of glacial activity, clothed in the work of humans.

Glacial Valley

The biggest change is caused by the Carrock End Fault, a geological faultline running north–south, cutting the limestone off and marking the rise of a new rock form – the Skiddaw slates.

Into this gap poured millennia of glacial ice, choking the valleys with a silty debris and sculpting their sides into still more vertiginous slopes. Mosedale takes its name from the Old Norse for valley of the bog (or moss), and it's these underlying factors of earth science that cause the Caldew to shoot out of the 'dale' part of Mosedale at a considerable pace, only to get sucked into the 'mose' part, where the raised bogs of Bowscale and Mosedale mosses draw it in and hold it.

Rich Ecology

The result is a valley where the water of the of the River Caldew turns sharp left to eventually reach the Eden near Carlisle, but a few paces to the right, the waters of the River Glenderamackin flow south then west to the Greta and Derwent, finally making the sea at Workington. Of all Lakeland's watersheds, this is possibly the most peculiar. You get several good glimpses of the mosses on this walk, without getting your feet too wet, hopefully. Mosedale and Bowscale mosses form a distinct Site of Special Scientific Interest, harbouring a rich bogland ecology, which is quite rare on a global scale.

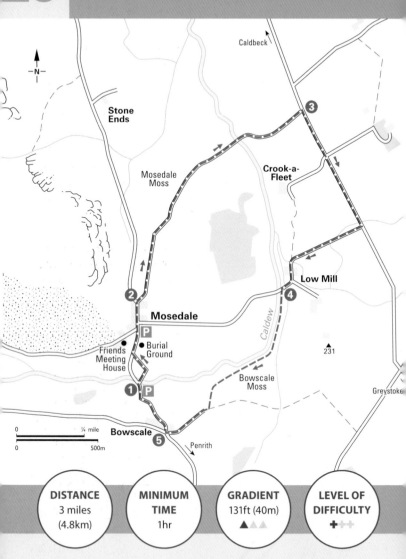

DISTANCE	MINIMUM TIME	GRADIENT	LEVEL OF DIFFICULTY
3 miles (4.8km)	1hr	131ft (40m) ▲▲▲	✚✚✚

PATHS Minor roads, farm tracks and grassy paths, some muddy, 5 stiles
LANDSCAPE Open marshland valley and farmland surrounded by rough fells
SUGGESTED MAP OS Explorer OL5 The English Lakes (NE) **START/FINISH** Grid reference: NY357319 **DOG FRIENDLINESS** A few road sections and sheep in the fields means you will have them on lead more often than not **PARKING** Parking area on south side of the Caldew bridge in Mosedale, or in Friends Meeting House car park (donation) **PUBLIC TOILETS** None on route, nearest in Keswick

WALK 29 DIRECTIONS

❶ From the parking area, walk over the old bridge and up the grassy lane beyond to reach the road. Turn right and walk into the hamlet of Mosedale, passing the Quaker Meeting House to the left with its ancient burial ground on the right (by the car park). Walk through the hamlet and opposite the last buildings (Mosedale End Farm) turn right, along a walled track signposted towards the River Caldew.

❷ Follow the track to a gate, beyond which it continues to the river. Cross by the footbridge and ascend the rough lane opposite, eventually to emerge at a T-junction with a minor road.

❸ Turn right and follow this for 400yds (366m) – ignoring the turning for Crook-a-Fleet – to a minor lane signposted for Low Mill. Turn right down the lane, following it as it threads between farm buildings. About 100yds (91m) beyond the turning for Low Mill Farm, as you approach a bridge across the Caldew, look for a gate into the field on the left.

❹ Go though this and follow the river bank levee, crossing a pair of stiles before being directed away from the river to the left and a stile and gate. Stay with the left-hand edge to another gate and stile, beyond which a rough track leads to a further gate and stile out on to a track heading out across Bowscale Moss. Turn right up this rough lane to reach the hamlet of Bowscale.

❺ At the junction with the road, turn right, following the road between the buildings and down the lane beyond, taking care as it narrows between hedges to return to your car.

ⓦ EATING AND DRINKING

In summer there are few places more serene or evocative than the volunteer-run tea rooms at the Friends Meeting House in Mosedale. At other times of the year, or if you're in need of something more substantial, the Mill Inn at Mungrisdale offers a full menu of bar and restaurant food, and keeps a good range of Robinson's beers.

🦆 ON THE WALK

In Mosedale you'll see the tiny burial ground associated with the Friends Meeting House. George Fox, founder of the Society of Friends, came to speak in Mosedale in 1653, and soon after there was an established meeting of local Quakers. There are no headstones in the burial ground, following the Quaker tradition, but the last interment was in 1921 and the site is no longer used for burial. The simple meeting house is up the lane on the left. It was built in 1702 and carefully restored by volunteers in the 1970s. Meetings are still held there today and in the summer months it houses a coffee shop.

LOW RIGG AND CASTLERIGG

At the heart of the northern Lakes, this simple walk begins at a lovely church and rounds to the inspiring stone circle at Castlerigg.

The stone circle at Castlerigg has been attracting tourists since the 17th century and featured in all the guidebooks that began to make the Lake District a destination from the 18th century onwards. It still retains the power to inspire, even on a dank day. There are 38 stones in a not-quite-round circle. Ten more form a little grove to one side.

Majestic Isolation

Some have suggested there is a relationship between this apparently secondary arrangement and the tumulus on the summit of Great Mell Fell, several miles to the east. One can draw an alignment of a solstice sunrise, apparently, though in an area surrounded by shapely mountains, many of which also boast ancient remains, the relationship may be coincidental. What is known about the circle is scant. It dates from the late-neolithic/early Bronze Age, perhaps 3000–2500 BC and it's one of a trio in the county that suggest there was a culture here of some sophistication. The other two – Long Meg and her Daughters near Langwathby and Swinside near Duddon Bridge – share Castlerigg's sense of majestic isolation, but beyond that there seems a great deal of conjecture. There hasn't even been a great deal of active archaeological investigation, though the National Trust did step in to 'rescue' Castlerigg as early as 1913 when there was a suggestion the stones may be fenced off and people charged for the privilege of walking among them. As recently as 2003 an axe, dateable to around 3000 BC, from the Langdale 'factory', was recovered from a nearby field.

Aged Stones

No amount of speculation detracts however from the grandeur of the place. The poet John Keats was clearly so impressed on his visit to the 'Druid Stones' in 1818 that it made up for a late dinner: 'We had to fag up the hill rather too close to dinner time, which was rendered void by the gratification of seeing those aged stones on a gentle rise in the midst of the mountains', he wrote to his brother the next day.

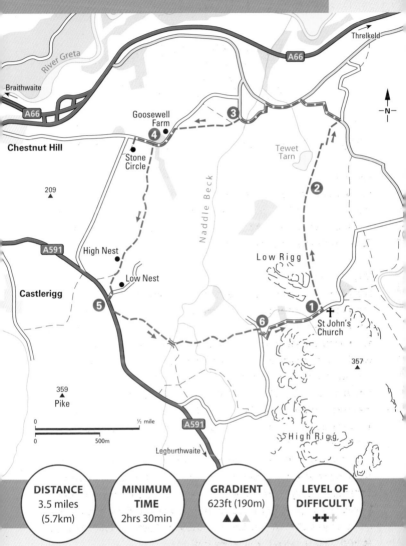

DISTANCE	MINIMUM TIME	GRADIENT	LEVEL OF DIFFICULTY
3.5 miles (5.7km)	2hrs 30min	623ft (190m) ▲▲△	╋╋╋

PATHS Grassy paths and tracks, a little road walking, 6 stiles **LANDSCAPE** Fell, fields and open valley **SUGGESTED MAP** OS Explorer OL4 The English Lakes (NW) **START/FINISH** Grid reference: NY 306224 **DOG FRIENDLINESS** Fields grazed by sheep so dogs should be under control throughout **PARKING** Responsibly around St John's Church and the Diocesan Youth Centre. Don't block the turning circle and note there is no onward access on the road beyond here, whatever SatNav might say! **PUBLIC TOILETS** None on route, nearest in Keswick (3 miles/4.8km)

WALK 30 DIRECTIONS

❶ Opposite the church, climb a stile, and follow the grassy path to the right around the marshland beyond, to a wall and stile. Go through a grassy gap until the tarn comes into view ahead and the stone circle at Castlerigg can be seen to the left beyond a white building in the distance. A broad grassy swathe leads down a gently sloping boggy field.

❷ A gate and stile leads you through a crossing fence and an obvious path continues to the right of the tarn and another gate and stile. Field paths now lead you on, eventually to meet a road. Turn left along the road and left again at a T-junction. At the next junction, turn left with the signs to the stone circle and climbing wall. Follow this loop of road across a beck and just beyond the bridge, take a turning on the left into fields.

❸ A rising path takes you over a stile and up through the fields to the road at the buildings of Goosewell Farm. Turn left along the road, passing the former farm buildings and climbing wall. As the road bends around to the right by a wood, look for a sign on the left to High Nest and the A591. Don't follow it but you'll come back to this point shortly.

❹ Continue along the road to the Castlerigg stone circle, accessed through a gate into the field on your left. Afterwards, return to the road and

> ### 🍴 EATING AND DRINKING
> Try the little Tea Garden at Low Bridge End Farm (Legburthwaite end of the Vale of St John) or the Horse and Farrier in Threlkeld.

turn right, descending to the path sign passed earlier. Go through the gate and follow the obvious field paths through to the farmhouse at High Nest. Past the restored barn, join the access road to a cattle grid. Here take the left turn signed towards the A591. Approaching the main road you pass through a gate to a cattle grid on the access road to Low Nest. Turn right and emerge on the verge of the busy A591.

❺ Turn left along the verge for a few paces to another footpath sign on the left. Go though the gate and descend the field to a stile. Keep left in the next field, following the boundary and at the bottom, go through the gateway, carrying on along a muddy farm track for 120yds (110m) to a footpath sign just over a little bridge. Turn left and follow the grassy line to a bridge over the Naddle Beck. On the far side continue though a gateway then across a field. Head for a kissing gate in a fence and make your way up the craggy bank, bearing slightly left up the hill. Another kissing gate leads out on to the notorious Old Coach Road.

❻ Turn left and walk up the track, following it all the way to the gate by the youth centre and the start.

WALKING
THE LINE

A lovely walk along a disused railway line is followed
by a return through the woods.

The railway line from Penrith to Cockermouth was the only one to actually
pass through this area, taking a deliberate line to Keswick in order to tap
into the tourist market. Opened to goods traffic in October 1864 and to
passengers two months later, the line was, however, built for industrial rather
than tourist reasons, to transport low phosphorous coke from Durham via
Stainmore to the iron foundries of west Cumberland.

Low Briery

One of the stops along the route was Low Briery, the site of an old bobbin
mill. In the early 19th century there was a water-powered pencil mill here,
several bobbin mills and a specialist textile mill, known locally as Fancy
Bottoms Mill, which made the intricate bottom edgings of waistcoats.

The earliest bobbin mills in Cumbria appeared during the Industrial
Revolution in response to demand from the mills of Lancashire and Yorkshire.
By the mid-19th century, there were some 120 water-powered bobbin mills
in the Lake District alone, producing half of all the bobbins required by
the entire world textile industry. Bobbins from Low Briery, which at peak
production could turn over 40 million bobbins a year, went as far as Central
America, South Africa and Hong Kong. There were many different types of
bobbin made at Low Briery, including those used for making the coronation
gown of Queen Elizabeth II. Other bobbins were used for silk, cotton, Irish
linen and the wire that was inserted into the old pound notes.

An End and a New Beginning

The arrival of the railway in 1864 meant that timber could be brought from
further away and made it easier for the growing workforce to reach the
mill. However, with the decline of the textile industry and competition from
abroad, the bobbin market collapsed, and Low Briery closed in 1961. By March
1972, the whole of this modest railway enterprise, too, came to an end. Much
of the route has since been incorporated into the A66 road, but some remains
as the Keswick Railway Footpath and a stretch of the National Cycle Network.

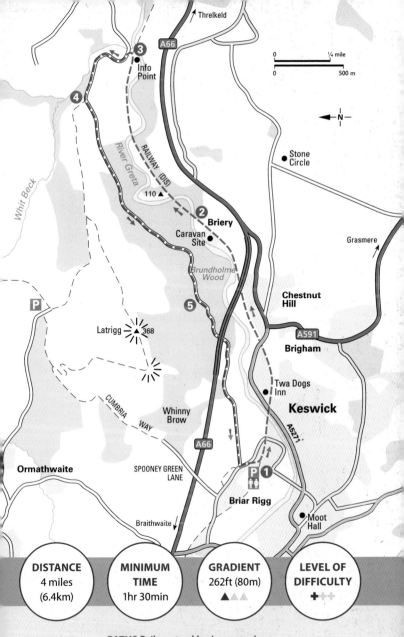

A66

3
Info
Point

4

River Greta

RAILWAY (DIS)

110 ▲

Whit Beck

Stone
Circle

2 Briery

Caravan
Site

*Brundholme
Wood*

Grasmere

Chestnut
Hill

A591

Brigham

5

[P]

Latrigg ▲ 368

Twa Dogs
Inn

Keswick

A5271

CUMBRIA
WAY

Whinny
Brow

A66

Ormathwaite

SPOONEY GREEN
LANE

[P] **1**

Braithwaite ↓

Briar Rigg

Moot
Hall

N

0 ¼ mile
0 500 m

DISTANCE	MINIMUM TIME	GRADIENT	LEVEL OF DIFFICULTY
4 miles (6.4km)	1hr 30min	262ft (80m) ▲▲▲	+++

PATHS Railway trackbed, country lane
LANDSCAPE River valley and woodland
SUGGESTED MAP OS Explorer OL4 The English Lakes (NW)
START/FINISH Grid reference: NY 270238
DOG FRIENDLINESS No particular problems, though look out for cyclists
PARKING At former Keswick Station
PUBLIC TOILETS At start

Opposite: River Greta flowing through Brundholme Wood, Keswick   Keswick **113**

WALK 31 DIRECTIONS

1 From the old Keswick Station, head along the trackbed, which speeds you away from Keswick. Beyond the A66, here cantilevered above the trackbed, the route covers a boardwalk section high above the River Greta, before continuing to the site of the bobbin mill at Low Briery, now a caravan site.

🍴 EATING AND DRINKING

The nearest place is the Twa Dogs Inn, shortly after the start – a pub name that comes from one of the poems of Robert Burns. Otherwise, head for Keswick, where there is a good choice of restaurants, cafés, snack bars and pubs.

🦢 ON THE WALK

A pair of binoculars would be a useful item to carry on this walk. The River Greta's fast-flowing waters are a habitat for many young invertebrates that live in the river for up to three years. This makes it popular with dippers, kingfishers and grey heron. In autumn and winter the fields and bushes alongside the river are visited by wintering thrushes – fieldfare and mistle thrush – and brambling.

2 Beyond Low Briery, the River Greta is an agreeable companion as far as an old railway building on the right used as an information point (with a river bridge beyond).

3 Before reaching the building, turn left through a gate and cross a narrow pasture to a quiet lane. Turn left and climb, steeply for a short while, to reach a footpath signed 'Skiddaw', at a gate and stile.

4 Don't go through this, but continue on the surfaced road, now heading back in the direction of Keswick. Shortly you'll pass a barrier closing the road to traffic. Stay on this winding woodland lane, through two sets of gates to another barrier by a forestry workers lay-by.

5 Continue along the lane, now with very occasional cars, over the A66 and past the Calvert Trust's equestrian centre. Stay on the lane to a junction and turn left to return to the parking areas around Keswick railway station.

🌿 IN THE AREA

Wander around Keswick, the largest town in the Lake District, and a place of lovely streets and buildings, the most prominent being the Moot Hall, now an information centre. It was built in 1813 on the site of an earlier building and was formerly the town hall ('moot' means 'to argue' or 'discuss'.) Keswick was once the centre of a copper mining industry and the world centre of the graphite and pencil industries. The town's famous pencil museum is worth a visit.

CALDBECK GREEN AND THE HOWK

Green fields give way to a riverside path
and a surprising little limestone gorge.

The Howk is surprising whichever way you approach it. This walk brings you in from the top end. The Whelpo Beck looks benign until it slips away into woodland and suddenly disappears over an edge into a chasm. No wonder the old folk called it the Fairy Kettle. Beside it the Fairy Kirk is a cave hollowed out of the limestone. It's a magical place deserving of a supernatural name. 'Howk' means scooping out in the old dialect of these northern fells, and it feels appropriate for this peculiar phenomenon – caused by a change in the underlying rock. This is a limestone gorge, a Gordale in miniature.

Auld Red Rover

Beyond, going downstream, is another surprise. No sooner than you have stepped away from the little shelf-like viewing area of the Howk, you are confronted by another oddity. The high, stone-built mill that blocks your passage was once the home of Auld Red Rover, in its time one of the largest waterwheels in the country. Over 17 tons of metal held this monster together. It was over 42ft (12.8m) in diameter and at full pelt turned barely three times in a minute. Built in 1857, Red Rover powered a bobbin mill, the rest of which is well preserved beyond the wheel pit. Here is the coppice shed, where the dressed poles of wood were stacked to dry, and the turning floors where skilled men would craft millions of bobbins to serve Lancashire's cotton mills.

Turned Goods

The Howk mill was in production until 1924, by which time the biggest cotton mills were making their own bobbins, and new materials were starting to replace the traditional wood. The Howk produced hundreds of different items too, from 'dolly pegs', for washing clothes in your 'dolly tub' to actual children's dollies, and the market for turned goods stretched beyond Manchester to Ireland and even Calcutta.

Caldbeck was a busy working village then, with mills and breweries and mines. Today it is a quiet place, but it is still worthwhile taking the time to explore the village at the end of your walk.

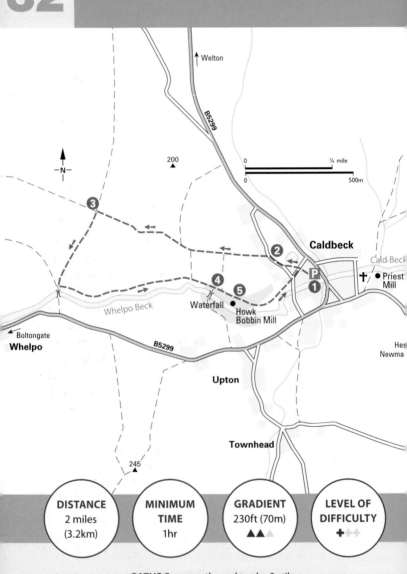

Welton ↑

B5299

200 ▲

0   ¼ mile

0   500m

–N–

3

2   **Caldbeck**

Cald-Beck

P

1   † ● Priest Mill

4   **5**

Waterfall   ● Howk Bobbin Mill

← Boltongate

Whelpo Beck

Whelpo

B5299

Hes Newma

Upton

Townhead

245 ▲

DISTANCE 2 miles (3.2km)	MINIMUM TIME 1hr	GRADIENT 230ft (70m) ▲▲▲	LEVEL OF DIFFICULTY ✚✚✚

PATHS Grassy paths and tracks, 3 stiles

LANDSCAPE Fields, riverside, limestone gorge and village green

SUGGESTED MAP OS Explorer OL5 The English Lakes (NE)

START/FINISH Grid reference: NY 322398

DOG FRIENDLINESS Fields grazed by sheep but alright by Whelpo Beck

PARKING Caldbeck car park, close to village green on north side of village

PUBLIC TOILETS On main street in Caldbeck village

WALK 32 DIRECTIONS

❶ Leave the parking area by the northern corner entrance, leading out onto the village green. Walk across the left-hand corner of the green to intersect the perimeter road and follow it right, away from the car park and pond. As the road swings right, look for a bridleway sign on the left to Faulds Brow.

❷ Follow this through a gate and up an enclosed track between hedgerows. Emerging into fields, ignore any turnings and keep straight ahead, shortly picking up an enclosed trackway again. Keep ahead with a wall on your right, going through a gate. Turn right to a gate and stile then bear left across a faint field path towards a gate on the opposite side. Through this, turn right heading for a gate at the top of the field. Bear half right up the hill beyond this, picking out an ancient sunken lane at the brow, weaving between trees to a small gate. In a few more paces you'll find a stile on the left.

❸ Cross this and walk across the bottom of a field to a kissing gate. Now descend with the wall, then a fence on your left. At the bottom, by the Whelpo Beck, turn left over a stone stile and follow the beckside path. The route narrows to step over a joining beck and pass through a kissing gate. A short flight of steps leads to another gate, where you bear right still heading downstream.

🍴 EATING AND DRINKING

There are several options in Caldbeck of which the pick is probably the Watermill Café at Priest's Mill. You'll find Fairtrade tea and coffee, home-made cakes, scones and gingerbread and more substantial things from sandwiches and ciabattas to Cumberland ham platters.

❹ As the beck twists away into trees, the path rises up the bank to a gate in a hedgerow. Now a narrow, enclosed path descends towards the sound of rushing water. Pass a waterfall and the path levels above a limestone gorge. A footbridge over the beck on the right affords a fine view of what is known as the Fairy Kettle. Don't cross the bridge, but continue to a flight of steep steps with more views into the gorge.

🚶 ON THE WALK

As you walk past the village green at the start of the walk, look for the duck pond down to your right. It's known as the 'Claydubs' and was once a clay pit, the clay used locally for making bricks and tiles.

❺ At the foot of the steps continue downstream, passing the ruins of the Howk bobbin mill. A level path leads back towards the village, swinging away from the beck and passing through a gated yard. Walk ahead toward the village green, turning right in a few paces to return to the car park.

OSPREYS OVER BASSENTHWAITE

A steep climb into the woods is rewarded by magnificent views and, if you're lucky, the glimpse of an osprey.

It's assumed that ospreys were extinct in England by 1840, and in Scotland by 1916. These graceful birds were persecuted for their audacity in daring to take fish from the lakes and streams of the landed classes. Their eggs were stolen by collectors and their migrations interrupted by southern European hunters. But in 1954 it was noticed that a breeding pair had returned to the Highlands of Scotland.

Breeding Ospreys

Probably from a Scandinavian ancestry, these new birds built their distinctive nests and slowly began to expand. But it was painfully slow. The Royal Society for the Protection of Birds (RSPB) at Loch Garten took an active role in protecting their nesting sites and even then, by 1976 there were only 14 breeding pairs. But the hard work of conservationists began to pay dividends. Twenty-four hour security for the nests helped fend off the egg thieves and by 1991 numbers had swelled to 71. With so many birds now making the long migration every year to West Africa, perhaps it was inevitable that some would find alternative places to breed, where competition for food was a bit less intense. In the mid 90s eagle-eyed Forestry Commission staff had noticed some birds were beginning to spend a little time each summer in the forests of Whinlatter, making their distinctive diving predatory fish grabs in the waters of Bassenthwaite Lake. A partnership between the Forestry Commission, the National Park and the RSPB was developed and the Osprey Project was born. In 2001 a pair bred at a nesting site in Thornthwaite Forest, the first in England for over 160 years and they have returned every year since.

To see them you'll have to be in the right place at the right time. That means being somewhere on the slopes of Dodd, the shapely forested mountain above Bassenthwaite's eastern shore, sometime between April and the end of August. You'll find staff at the viewing stations with binoculars and telescopes to help you, and if you miss out, you can always watch the day's highlights on TV up at the Whinlatter visitor centre. Ospreys are big business in this valley, but still a dramatic sight for all that.

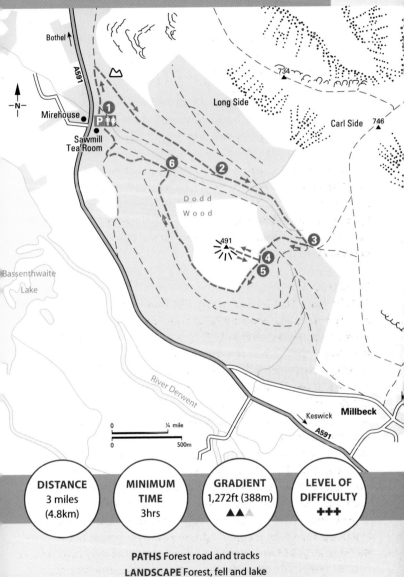

DISTANCE
3 miles
(4.8km)

MINIMUM TIME
3hrs

GRADIENT
1,272ft (388m)
▲▲▲

LEVEL OF DIFFICULTY
+++

PATHS Forest road and tracks
LANDSCAPE Forest, fell and lake
SUGGESTED MAP OS Explorer OL4 The English Lakes (NW)
START/FINISH Grid reference: NY 234281
DOG FRIENDLINESS Good for dogs
PARKING Dodd Wood Sawmill car park
PUBLIC TOILETS At car park

WALK 33 DIRECTIONS

❶ From the car park at The Old Sawmill Tearoom, cross the bridge and follow the sign marked 'All Trails'. Cut back left with the multicoloured trail marker and stay with these on a route heading back towards the road before cutting back into the woods to a junction. Cross to the path on the opposite side, now heading up less steeply. At a junction in front of a wooded crag turn right, continuing to ascend with red, green and blue trails. Climbing relentlessly, the path rises through the forest. Ignore the blue trail dropping off to the right (unless you've had enough already!) and continue now with just read and green on a more level path. Cross a beck and keep ahead, rising through an area of beech wood before descending to join a trail rising up from the valley below.

❷ Turn left along this and stay with it past a junction on your right where the red and green route turns off. The track, with fading tarmac, enters a clear felled area and continues up the valley, now as a rougher forest track. At a craggy junction with a forest road from the left, continue ahead, keeping this direction past another junction with a track joining from the right. You've rejoined the green trail now heading for another junction at the col ahead.

❸ Turn right here on the path directed to Dodd summit. It swings round the shoulder and a high balcony path gently edges up the slope. Rounding another bend a series of green posts lead left and right.

❹ Take the right-hand option, up a zig-zagging path that in time tops out at the summit by a memorial cairn. Don't be tempted to follow the ridge onward from here, instead, after soaking up the view, return to the junction passed earlier with the green post options. Now take the second option, walking out to a belvedere viewpoint.

❺ In a dip just before it, a narrow path nips away to the right, soon revealing itself as your descent route. The zig-zag path brings you speedily down though young plantations before settling to a more gradual slide into more mature forest. Stay with green-topped posts as the path steepens then emerges on a wider trail. Turn right, along this trail descending steadily, turning left to rejoin the red markers again.

❻ Keep ahead though at the next junction on the larger track, ignoring the red and green trail dropping down to the right. Reaching a wider forest road, turn right and follow it immediately swinging left. At the next junction, you'll find the osprey viewpoint a few paces down the track to the left. To return to the tea room, turn right here and follow the osprey marker posts soon rejoining the red and green posts at a crossroads and keeping on down to the car park.

BINSEY'S FAR AWAY HEIGHTS

This distant outpost of the Lakeland fells makes for a lovely circular ramble with grand views all around.

Binsey is not often on the itinerary of the casual visitor to the Lake District, but pick a good day for this gentle walk, perhaps when the northern Lakes are feeling a bit crowded, and you will be rewarded with exceptional vistas.

The geology of Binsey is different from the Skiddaw massif that bulks up its horizon to the north. Skiddaw, and the high, rolling fells that once made up its hunting forest, have a rock name to themselves. Skiddaw slate, a hard, metamorphosed sedimentary rock is green in colour and can be seen in nearly every building in Keswick. Binsey's origins are volcanic, being largely made of basaltic andesite and rhyolite from a group rocks known as the Eycott group. Eycott is a very unprepossessing hill – blink by the Troutbeck turn on the A66 and you will have missed it on the right.

According to computerised imagery, the view from the summit of Binsey on a clear day should extend to the tip of Slieve Donard, a mere 115 miles (185km) away across the Irish Sea. It would seem to be optimistic perhaps. What is more noticeable, this far north in the Cumbrian peninsula, is the proximity of Criffel, just over the Solway. From this far north-western summit, the top of Dumfries's favourite hill is actually closer to hand than the Pennines.

Devastating Floods

Directly south, Bassenthwaite Lake curves gracefully up to Keswick, and Derwent Water beyond spreads before a fine background of high fells – Scafell Pike, the Langdales, Great Gable, Grisedale Pike can all be seen. To the west the Derwent Valley chugs gently down towards Cockermouth, Workington and the sea. This is a good spot to appreciate the vast extent of the River Derwent's catchment. On that fateful day in November 2009, over 12in (300mm) of rain fell on Seathwaite, at the head of Borrowdale, in 24 hours. Joined by waters from Thirlmere and the valley below you, it swept down the vale, meeting more torrents from Buttermere at one end of Cockermouth's Main Street. Tragically, one person died that day, but from these heights you'll be amazed that the floods didn't claim more victims.

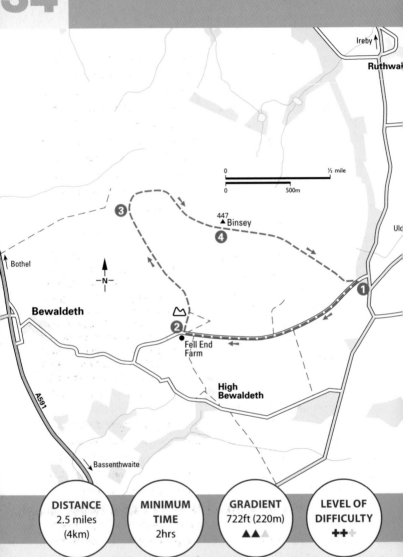

DISTANCE	MINIMUM TIME	GRADIENT	LEVEL OF DIFFICULTY
2.5 miles (4km)	2hrs	722ft (220m) ▲▲▲	++++

PATHS Road, moorland paths and tracks **LANDSCAPE** Upland farms and moorland **SUGGESTED MAP** OS Explorer OL4 The English Lakes (NW) **START/FINISH** Grid reference: NY 235350 **DOG FRIENDLINESS** Fields grazed by cattle, otherwise reasonably suitable for dogs **PARKING** At roadside pull-in on a minor road near to Binsey Lodge, off the Ireby to Castle Inn road **PUBLIC TOILETS** None on route

WALK 34 DIRECTIONS

❶ From the roadside parking area, walk down the quiet lane. There is very little traffic here and ample space at the side of the road to avoid it, but do keep an ear open for oncoming traffic.

❷ In a mile (1.6km) or so you'll come to the farmyard at Fell End, where you should turn right, through a gate by a well. In the steep field beyond, stay initially with the left-hand boundary before striking off on a similar line towards a gate in the wall at the head of the field. You'll find it more convenient to pick the blue left-hand gate of the two you may be able to see. Through the gate, turn left soon picking up a narrow trod contouring around the fell, initially about 10 paces up from the wall, then maintaining its height as the wall slips away to the left. Continue on this line, indistinct in places but always traceable, eventually beginning to round the flank of the fell.

❸ A lone blackthorn tree marks a path junction. Turn right here heading up the fell, briefly stepping over a small beck where the path divides to continue up into a boggy valley below the rocks of West Crag. Rounding a bend the track becomes more substantial and is joined by a track rising up from the left. Continue upwards, the gradient now easing, ignoring paths off to left and right. At last the summit cairn comes in to view straight ahead.

> 🍴 **EATING AND DRINKING**
> The Snooty Fox at Uldale (about 2 miles/3.2km north-east of Binsey on the Caldbeck road) serves good food and local beer. There's a fine beer garden round the back with views up to the fell. It isn't open at lunchtimes however and there's no food on Wednesdays. Well-behaved dogs and children are tolerated.

❹ Walk up to its rocky shelter, then walk off maintaining your previous direction, heading for the dark tarn of Overwater in the valley below. A wide grassy path soon begins to descend through the heather, finally bringing you down to a gate in the wall adjacent to the roadside parking area.

> 🔎 **IN THE AREA**
> This is a quiet part of the National Park with a number of pretty settlements. Ireby, to the north of Binsey, clearly shows its origins as a medieval market town, with houses set around a square, though one suspects it was never terribly successful. Ireby's old church lies a mile (1.6km) or so out of the village, surrounded by fields. Built in the 13th century it was replaced in the 1840s and is now cared for by the Churches Conservation Trust.

WITH ROGUE HERRIES OVER GRANGE FELL

From Judith Paris's cottage in Watendlath
to one of the finest views in the Lake District.

One stormy night in 1739, Francis 'Rogue' Herries brought his family to live in the house his grandfather built in Borrowdale. His son, David, 'woke again to see that all the horses were at a standstill and were gathered about a small stone bridge.' The 'hamlet… clustered beyond the bridge' was probably Grange. From there they crossed over a hill to come at last 'into a little valley, as still as a man's hand and bleached under the moon, but guarded by a ring of mountains that seemed to David gigantic.' This is the village of Rosthwaite and the Hazel Bank hotel sits on the spot where the Herries house stood. However, this house never existed except in the imagination of the novelist Hugh Walpole (1884–1941) and between the covers of the four volume series he wrote, collectively known as *The Herries Chronicle* (1930–33).

The Herries Family Saga

Walpole, one of the best-selling writers of his day, wrote over 50 novels. He bought a house above Derwent Water in 1923 and two years later announced that he was 'pinning all my hopes on two or three Lakes' novels, which will at least do something for this adorable place.' What he eventually produced was a romantic history of a Lake District family from 1730 to 1932.

'Rogue' Herries, soon notorious in Borrowdale for his wildness, completes his infamy by selling his mistress at a fair. His consuming, unrequited love for Mirabell Starr, a gypsy woman, drives him to wander the country in search of her. Finally at Rosthwaite, after 44 years in Borrowdale, he dies as Judith, the daughter of his old age, is born in 1774.

Glorious View

From the summit of King's How there is a glorious view to the north over Derwent Water to Keswick and Skiddaw. Closer, in the plain of the River Derwent, with the steep sides of Cat Bells and High Spy rising behind, lies the tiny hamlet of Grange, where in the first of the Herries chronicles, 'Rogue' Herries lifted from the water the body of the old woman they had drowned as a witch. The bridge from which they threw her is visible.

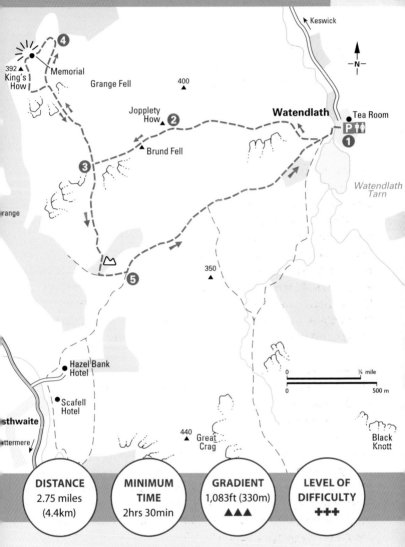

WALK 35 DIRECTIONS

❶ From the bottom of the car park go through the gate and past Fold Head Farm, the fictional home of Judith Paris. Turn right and make for the little bridge, turning left on the far side to meet up with a much larger track. Continue for a few paces to a junction of tracks by a fingerpost to Rosthwaite and Dock Tarn. Ignore both options but pick up a faint path to the right, leading up to a gate in the wall. Go through this and continue up a narrow path between crags to a boggy area. Keep a wall on your right as you ascend towards Jopplety How.

❷ When you reach a crossing wall, bear left to locate a single ladder stile (if you find a pair of single step stiles you're too far to the right). Cross the ladder stile and continue around Jopplety How and up to the rocky little summit of Brund Fell. Beyond this, descend to a T-junction.

❸ Turn right and descend on an obvious path, crossing a wall by a ladder stile. Cross another stile over a fence and turn right, along the edge of a boggy valley.

> ### ✦ IN THE AREA
> The single-track road to Watendlath from the Keswick to Borrowdale road is one of the most scenic in the Lake District. Half-way up you'll cross Ashness Bridge, with the much pictured backdrop of distant lakes and mountains. Beyond this on the right as you go up the road in the woods you'll find 'Surprise View'– don't go too near the edge!

❹ At the far side, by a prominent yew tree, turn left and follow a rocky path that ascends the ridge of King's How. Pass the memorial to King Edward VII and continue over the summit, before descending on the far side, first along the ridge then dropping down to the left, back to the stile crossed earlier. Retrace your steps up to the T-junction and continue straight on, eventually descending very steeply by a wood to a gated stile. Over this turn left and ascend briefly to another gate, leading out on to the main Rosthwaite bridleway.

❺ Turn left and follow this prominent track over Puddingstone Bank and back down to Watendlath.

> ### ⦿ EATING AND DRINKING
> The number one choice has to be lunch in the tea room at Watendlath, where, on a fine day, you can eat outside. A mug of hot chocolate, sheltering inside from the rain here is also always a pleasure. Otherwise there is a fine tea room beneath Shepherd's Crag near the Lodore Hotel, or you may find it easier to drive into nearby Keswick.

LANGSTRATH'S HIDDEN VALLEY

A low-level ramble into one of Lakeland's secret valleys, with waterfalls and high crags all around.

Study a map of Stonethwaite, and the Langstrath and Greenup valleys that meet barely 10 minutes' pleasant walk from the village's fine pub, and one name will usually leap out at you from the jumble of thwaites and becks and gills and fells. There, beneath Alisongrass Crag, stands Alisongrass Hoghouse. When you get there you'll find a small stone building, now converted to holiday accommodation, but its name and location can tell us lots about how farming in this valley used to work. But what about the hoghouse? Is this where the old farmers kept pigs? Not exactly. A hogg is a year old sheep, one of last year's lambs if you like, and the hoghouse ('hoggus') was where they were over-wintered.

Herdwick Sheep

Stonethwaite can trace its farming records to its days as an outpost of Fountains Abbey in the 14th century. That huge Yorkshire house of Cistercians produced vast quantities of wool, most of which was sold to itinerant Italian merchants. To understand the scale of the operation, Furness Abbey, the great rival to Fountains Abbey, and which also held land in Borrowdale (the village of Grange was their 'grange') sold 76 sacks of wool to one Snr Pergolitti in 1315. A sack weighs 364lbs (165kg), so it is estimated that this was the product of over 20,000 sheep!

The hoggs would be fed on straw and holly and often ash leaves over the winter time, before being taken back up to the fells to join the 'wedders' the castrated males that had been left to fend for themselves all winter. The Herdwick sheep proved perfectly suited to this form of production, and it wasn't until the end of the 18th century that they began to be wintered on grazing pastures lower down the valley instead of in hoghouses. Their distinctive grey fleeces were renowned as a wool that repelled water, and at the height of Fountains' production in the early 16th century, they accounted for 8 per cent of the monks' total wool output.

So Alisongrass Hoghouse is a peculiar name, but its story is also the story of this valley.

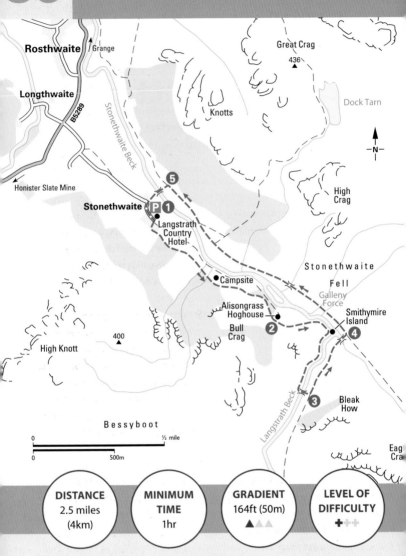

Rosthwaite / Grange

Longthwaite

B5289

Honister Slate Mine

Stonethwaite

Langstrath Country Hotel

Campsite

Alisongrass Hoghouse

Bull Crag

High Knott

400

Bessyboot

Great Crag

436

Knotts

Dock Tarn

High Crag

Stonethwaite

Fell

Galleny Force

Smithymire Island

Bleak How

Eag Cra

Langstrath Beck

Stonethwaite Beck

—N—

0   ½ mile

0   500m

DISTANCE	MINIMUM TIME	GRADIENT	LEVEL OF DIFFICULTY
2.5 miles (4km)	1hr	164ft (50m) ▲▲▲	+++

PATHS Stony tracks and paths, 2 stiles **LANDSCAPE** Village, woods, fields, fell
SUGGESTED MAP OS Explorer OL4 The English Lakes (NE)
START/FINISH Grid reference: NY 262137 **DOG FRIENDLINESS** Sheep grazing
country, so dogs should be on lead after Alisongrass Hoghouse
PARKING Small car park in Stonethwaite village by the phone box, or park on
the roadside back along the valley road. Please don't park in the pub car park
PUBLIC TOILETS None on route, nearest in Seatoller

WALK 36 DIRECTIONS

❶ Walk through Stonethwaite village, passing the Langstrath Country Hotel and continuing on the track to the right as it splits. Follow the brief tarmac continuation up a bank and on, soon reverting to a rough track. Beyond the entrance to the campsite stay on the track though a gate and you'll find it narrows to traverse a woody shoulder. Down the other side it rounds to a building on the left – Alisongrass Hoghouse.

Ⓜ IN THE AREA

Visit the Honister Slate Mine, perhaps for an exciting scramble on one of Britain's few 'via ferrata' (an assisted scrambling and climbing route) or for a guided walk into the heart of the mountain to see where the slate has been won for generations. There's a shop and a café as well.

❷ Continue into open country, turning left to pick up a riverside path beside the roar of Galleny Force. Continue on this path, crossing a stile and swinging to the right, where there's a chance to cross to the 'island' viewpoint and picnic spot known as Smithymire. Otherwise walk up to another stile and an onward path up the valley. Soon you rejoin your original lane and follow it further on through woodlands into Langstrath proper. Round a corner and go through a gate, soon reaching a footbridge on the left.

🍴 EATING AND DRINKING

The Langstrath Country Hotel is an excellent point for a pre- or post-walk meal and drink. There's a varied menu and good beer, but it gets busy in high season so you may have to book. Across the lane is an attractive beer garden.

❸ Turn left again on the far side and follow the path down the opposite bank, downstream. Pass through a gate and reach a second bridge opposite Smithymire Island.

❹ At the gate at the top of the bank, turn left, down the valley. Follow the obvious track through another gate, with a wall on either side. Opposite the campsite, pass through another gate and soon cross another footbridge. Maintain your direction through more gates until you reach a junction.

❺ Turn left, through another gate and over a bridge to join a farm track leading back into the centre of Stonethwaite.

🚶 ON THE WALK

The obvious thing to keep an eye open for is the hoghouses. Alisongrass is easy to spot by the side of the track, but you may see the remnants of others, particularly on the return leg, tucked in against the foot of the fell overlooking their former enclosures.

SIMPLY
CAT BELLS

A delightful romp high above some of Lakeland's loveliest scenery culminates in views over Derwent Water.

Cat Bells is arguably the best known of the lower Lakeland fells: certainly it is one of the most distinctive, its attractive conical shape gracing the western shores of Derwent Water. Many a first step to fell-walking exploration was planted on the grassy slopes of Cat Bells, a summit that remains ever popular for its outstanding views.

The great expanse of Derwent Water lies directly below, while to the north the slate slopes of Skiddaw dominate the market town of Keswick. Further right, the southern ridges of Blencathra overlook Glenderamackin Vale. To the east the Dodds lead into the Helvellyn range, while to the west graceful fells tumble along the skyline from Lord's Seat, across Grisedale Pike and Eel Crags to the high ground above unseen Buttermere beyond Robinson, Hindscarth and Dale Head.

Early Industry

Both Borrowdale and the Newlands Valley, like many parts of Lakeland, have seen extensive periods of industry from an early age. Copper was mined here as early as the 13th century from a vein 9ft (2.7m) thick. The mines also produced large quantities of lead, a small amount of silver and a modicum of gold. The mines' greatest period of production was in the 16th century, when Elizabeth I made a serious attempt to exploit England's own resources to reduce dependency on imports. Ironically, it was German miners who largely worked here, encouraged by the award of hidden subsidies in the form of waived taxes. Copper ore was taken by packhorse to the shores of Derwent Water by way of Little Town. It was then transported to a smelter on the banks of the River Greta, at Brigham. From here the copper went to the Receiving House, now the Moot Hall, in Keswick, to receive the Queen's Mark.

The northernmost of the lake's islands, Derwent Isle was the base of the German miners. They were not universally popular in Keswick and were quartered here for their own safety. St Herbert's Island is traditionally the site of a hermitage, and was the inspiration for Owl Island in Beatrix Potter's *The Tale of Squirrel Nutkin* (1903).

Opposite: View toward Latrigg and Keswick from Cat Bells

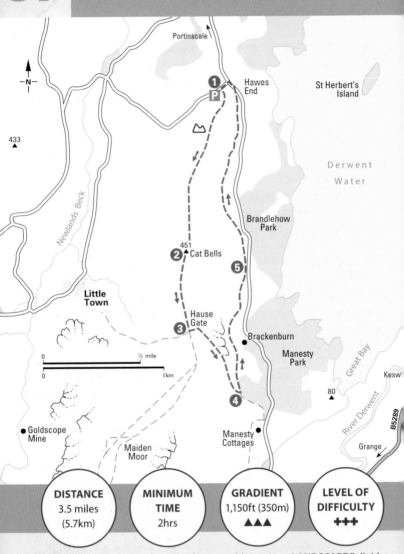

WALK 37 DIRECTIONS

❶ From the eastern end of the little parking area on the Skelgill road, take a narrow path leading up the bank then levelling off to skirt the fell. Soon it intersects with a more prominent path running up the hill – the main Cat Bells ridge path. It's stepped and rocky and rises steeply. Follow it, climbing through small rocky outcrops before reaching Brandlehow. The onward route keeps to the centre of a grassy ridge, before rising through more rock outcrops to the summit of Cat Bells.

❷ From Cat Bells descend easily to the broad col of Hause Gate.

Ⓘ IN THE AREA

Take a tour around the lake with Keswick Launch. Their regular ferry service connects a series of piers from Nichol End round to Barrow Bay and is great way to see the hills and woods from a different perspective. For an interesting day out, you could leave your car in Keswick and get the ferry to Hawse End to start the walk.

---

❸ Turn left on a clear path, and descend a constructed pathway towards the wooded area around Manesty. The path is awkward in places, especially near the top, but lower down broadens into a wide track. Keep descending to meet a path going left along the edge of woodland. (There are two earlier, higher shortcuts that meet this path, though the higher of the two requires care in wet conditions.) Turn left and follow the path above the woodland and the attractively set house of Brackenburn.

🍴 EATING AND DRINKING

Grange Bridge Cottage Tea Room in the village of Grange offers a range of teas and snacks throughout the year (reduced opening hours in winter).

---

❹ Beyond Brackenburn the footpath, which affords lovely views of Derwent Water, soon dips to make a brief acquaintance with the road at a small quarry car park.

❺ Beyond this gap, immediately return to a gently rising path. This is an old road, traversing the lower slopes of Cat Bells and it will ultimately bring you back to the road at Hawes End. Turn left to return to the Skelgill car park.

🚶 ON THE WALK

Brackenburn, below Hause Gate on the Derwent Water side, was the home of Hugh Walpole (1884–1941), the English novelist, born in New Zealand, who bought the property in 1923. His collection of works known as *The Herries Chronicle* (1930–33) is set in and around Borrowdale. Along the path above his home is a bench set before a memorial plaque marking a favoured spot with a stunning view across Derwent Water below.

RANNERDALE'S PECULIAR BLUEBELLS

An airy ridge walk along Rannerdale Knotts leads to a very unusual open fellside, famous for its bluebells in May.

This curiuos little mountain is worth the effort at most times of the year. The rugged face it sets against the valley of Crummock Water looks unassailable until you find a winding staircase of grass and rock steps, breaching its craggy summit after only a relatively short burst of exertion. Even in low cloud this creates an exhilarating experience of loftiness. On clear days the view is magnificent. Crummock Water's depths below the end of Rannerdale's crags plunge to over 70ft (21.3m) barely 8ft (2.4m) from the road.

Nicholas Size

But the road disarms Rannerdale Knotts of its most dramatic power – that of a barrier to the secret valley of Buttermere beyond. This at least was the theory developed by Nicholas Size (1866–1953), who once ran the Buttermere (now the Bridge) Hotel in the village. Size, a former railwayman, forsook his life as the Goods Manager at the old Bradford Exchange Station to become an outspoken proponent of tourist 'development' in the valley.

Secret Valley

Size is not remembered by posterity as an eccentric hotelier, but as an author. He was captivated by the absence of historical records about the area, particularly before the Normans exerted effective control in the 12th century. There were folk tales, and of course the place names, with their Norse and Celtic origins. Size set about putting some flesh on the stories and in *The Secret Valley* (1930) created a historical novella using the backdrop of his valley as a storyline. Earl Bothar, the last of the Celtic warrior chiefs defends his homeland from Norman invaders, coming up the dale from their castle at Cockermouth. Faced with the barrier of Rannerdale Knotts, the British lure their attackers into the dead end valley to the north, before descending on them from the surrounding heights in a massacre. It's gripping stuff, and the book sold in vast quantities to a 1930s public keen to read of resistance to foreign invaders. The bluebells that flourish on Rannerdale's open fellsides are supposed to have grown up from the corpses of the Norman invaders.

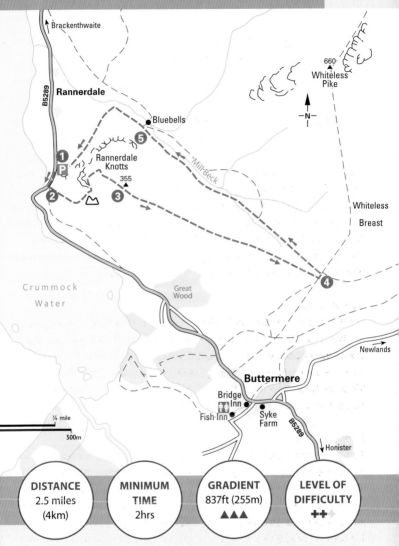

DISTANCE	MINIMUM TIME	GRADIENT	LEVEL OF DIFFICULTY
2.5 miles (4km)	2hrs	837ft (255m) ▲▲▲	++

PATHS Steep rocky paths, grassy paths and tracks
LANDSCAPE Steep fellside, open fell, valley and lake
SUGGESTED MAP OS Explorer OL4 The English Lakes (NW)
START/FINISH Grid reference: NY 163183
DOG FRIENDLINESS Fields grazed by sheep, reasonably suitable for dogs
PARKING Roadside lay-by near start
PUBLIC TOILETS In Buttermere village

WALK 38 DIRECTIONS

❶ With your back to the parking area turn left along the road for a few paces to a footpath sign on the left. Here you'll find a steep, pitched path that begins a snaking ascent of the precipitous slope.

❷ At a junction, take the left-hand steeper option and continue upwards through the bracken, soon reaching a grassy knoll with views of Buttermere and Crummock Water in the valley below. The path zigs back to the left and continues, joining a flight of rocky steps through a rocky ravine. As the grassy slopes return you are confronted by a pair of crags looming ahead. Your upward path is deflected to the right, emerging on a grassy shoulder before bearing right to the summit. The slightly underwhelming highest point is made worthwhile by taking a few paces towards the edge to reveal a magnificent vista up and down the valley.

❸ Follow the obvious ridge path, which includes one awkward rocky section before settling down to become an airy high level route across a series of bracken coated grassy knolls. As you approach the final humps, a short cut drops down to the left, but completists will want to carry on to the end of the ridge, where it terminates at a grassy col above the valley of Mill Beck beneath Whiteless Breast.

> ### 🌿 ON THE WALK
> In May, Rannerdale is famous for its bluebells. These delightful woodland flowers grow in super abundance on the bare fellside, an incongruity that clearly inspired generations of storytellers. The truth is more prosaic. The fellside here was probably still wooded until the 18th-century and the plants are a hangover from those days.

❹ Turn sharp left here on the prominent valley path that now mirrors your high level outward journey. Follow the path all the way down to a gate in a wall corner by a footbridge.

❺ In spring it's worth crossing here to immerse yourself in the fellside bluebells, but at other times of the year, continue on the left-hand side of the beck on a path that clings to the foot of the fell, soon swerving off to the left away from the beck. Pass through a kissing gate and continue with a wall now on your right to emerge at the back of the little parking area.

> ### 🍴 EATING AND DRINKING
> There's a good choice at Buttermere village including the Bridge Inn (Nicholas Size's 'Buttermere Hotel') and the Fish Inn. Syke Farm produces its own delicious ice cream and boasts a delightful, recently built café space.

GETTING HIGH ON LONELY LOWESWATER

Discovering Lakeland's finest balcony in a peaceful and little-trodden corner of the north-western fells.

Loweswater's a bit of a thief: it steals the best views of Crummock Water's fells – Grasmoor and Whiteside never looked more fair than they do from Carling Knott's balcony path, and little Mellbreak bursts into the sky like a volcano – with its steep and rocky slopes.

Following the Corpse Road
Loweswater village is little more than the Kirkstile Inn, the church and the village hall, with a scattering of whitewashed farm buildings in the lush green fields and alongside the narrow country lanes. The walk starts on the outskirts of the village, by Maggie's Bridge. It uses an old corpse road to get to the fellsides. The corpses? They would have been parishioners from Loweswater, for the church didn't have its own burial ground. They would be strapped on to horses' backs before being carried all the way to St Bees on the coast. After the climb up the high sides of Carling Knott, the mourners might not have appreciated that this is one of the most splendid balcony paths in Cumbria – green, flat and true – and with wonderful views across the lake to Darling Fell.

To Farmland and Lake
The old track descends towards farm pastures. The names of the farmhouses – Iredale Place, Jenkinson Place and Hudson Place – are all derived from the original owners' names. But we break off early, into the National Trust's Holme Wood and the secret Holme Beck waterfall. Oak predominates near the lake, although the trees at the top of the wood largely consist of pine, larch and Sitka spruce. This isn't natural woodland, having been planted in the last hundred years or so. The wood is one of the last strongholds of the red squirrel. You're very likely to see pied and spotted flycatchers here, and maybe, if you're lucky, a green woodpecker.

The path leaves the lake behind, comes out of the woods and crosses the fields of Watergate, back to Maggie's Bridge. Mellbreak still towers above the trees, tauntingly, tantalisingly showing off its scree paths to the summit. Another day perhaps, for this has been a day for quiet contemplation.

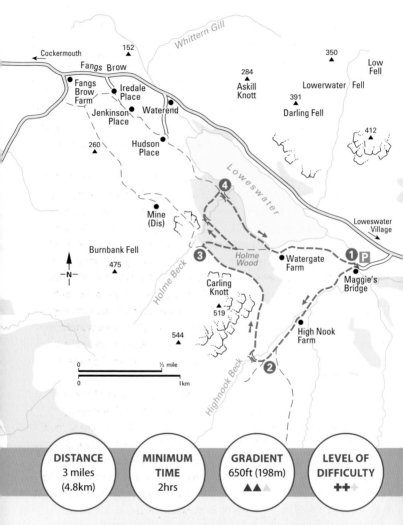

DISTANCE
3 miles
(4.8km)

MINIMUM TIME
2hrs

GRADIENT
650ft (198m)
▲▲▲

LEVEL OF DIFFICULTY
+++

PATHS Well-defined paths and tracks, all stiles have adjacent gates
LANDSCAPE Hillside, farm pastures, forest and lakes
SUGGESTED MAP OS Explorer OL4 The English Lakes (NW)
START/FINISH Grid reference: NY 134210 **DOG FRIENDLINESS** On lead, except
for Holme Wood **PARKING** Maggie's Bridge car park, Loweswater (get there early)
PUBLIC TOILETS None on route, nearest at National Park car park
in Buttermere (3 miles/4.8km)

WALK 39 DIRECTIONS

❶ Just opposite the car park entrance go through the gate to High Nook Farm and follow the track through the fields. After passing through the farmyard continue along a stony track that climbs into the comb of Highnook Beck and beneath the craggy sides of Carling Knott.

❷ Take the right fork each time the path divides. This will bring you down to the footbridge across the beck. Across the bridge the route continues as a grassy track that doubles back right, raking across the hillside to the top of the Holme Wood plantations. The track follows the top edge of the woods, passing through a gate at the

---

🐾 ON THE WALK

One thing you may notice on your visit to Loweswater is that it outflows not to the lowlands, but towards the high fells – the only lake in Cumbria to do this.

---

highest point where there is a view of the Solway and the Scottish coast.

❸ Descend for another 100yds (91m), but as the path begins to head round the valley of Holme Beck, look right for a kissing gate into the plantation. Through this a descending track cuts back right, through the woods, to a junction with a larger forestry track. Turn left here, taking a more gentle downward direction, soon crossing Holme Beck where there is a bridge and a waterfall. Eventually you will meet a good track at a T-junction.

❹ Turn right, recrossing Holme Beck by a bridge and ford. Keep straight ahead at a path junction just beyond a stone-built bunkhouse. Through a gate approaching Watergate Farm, turn left on a grassy path that soon rejoins the wide gravel road back to the car park at Maggie's Bridge.

🍴 EATING AND DRINKING

The Kirkstile Inn at Loweswater is one of the best in the Lakes. It serves good-value, high-quality food – a succulent steak with a green peppercorn and mustard sauce is complemented by an extensive, but reasonably priced wine list. Dogs are welcomed in the bar but not in the restaurant. Oak-beamed ceilings and an open fire make this an inviting place after a day on the hills.

🌿 IN THE AREA

There's been a place of worship at Loweswater since 1158 when Ranulph de Lyndesay gave a chapel and some land to the Abbey of St Bees. In 1827 that building was demolished to make way for the present much larger church, for lead mining had increased the local population to over 500 at this time. At the same time a school for 80 children was built – it's now the village hall.

THE WILDING OF ENNERDALE

A short walk dips a toe into this magnificent valley,
the home of an ambitious conservation project.

The big idea for a change or 'rewilding' in Ennerdale came from a change
in English forestry strategy in 1998. The Forestry Commission, charged
since 1919 with protecting the nation's timber reserves, found their wood
was no longer in competitive demand. No longer needed for pit props or
railway sleepers, other timber users found imports both cheaper and more
convenient. So the Forestry Commission was told to look at other priorities.
In Ennerdale this gave them an opportunity to right a few wrongs. Writing in
1966, famous fell-wandering author Alfred Wainwright described the valley's
afforestation as 'a dark and funereal shroud…an intrusion that nobody who
knew Ennerdale of old can ever forgive.' (*The Western Fells*, 1966). He was
equally scathing about the water board men who demolished one of the
valley's few pubs to raise the water level and then never actually did it.

Quiet Experiment

Water extraction and forestry aside, Ennerdale was quite clean underneath.
The records show that native woodland had been largely cleared by the end
of the 15th century and sheep and cattle grazing was as important here as
elsewhere. But there wasn't the same intensive valley use you might find
in Buttermere or Langdale. There was a medieval iron founder's bloomery
at Smithy Beck, and a larger settlement of Norse-style longhouses at
Gillerthwaite, but not much more. So the scope for repositioning the valley as
a quiet experiment in habitat change was clear.

The Wild Ennerdale project brings together the water company, the
forestry people and those who have interests in the valley. The plan is to
reduce the use of vehicles, particularly in the upper valley; to foster the
growth of native trees, and control the regeneration of introduced ones like
Sitka spruce; to let go of the margins of the woods, so they become less well-
defined; to lessen the impact of water extraction by removing revetments
and the like; and to use the whole valley as an educational tool, showing how
ecology and the environment is shaped by our actions. It's a bold and exciting
initiative – even Wainwright might have approved.

Opposite: View over green fields to Ennerdale Water

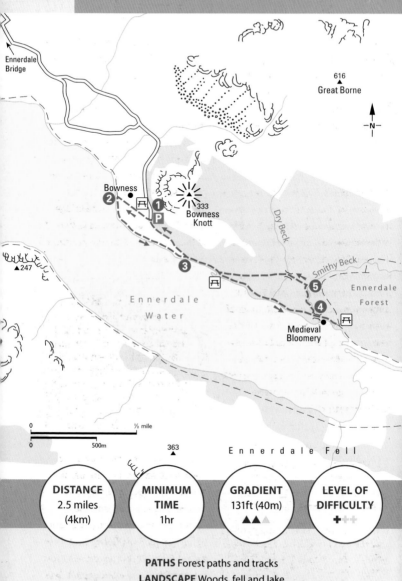

Ennerdale
Bridge

616 ▲
Great Borne

↑
—N—

Bowness
2
1 P
☀ 333
Bowness
Knott

Dry Beck

3

Smithy Beck

5

Ennerdale
Forest

▲247

E n n e r d a l e
W a t e r

4

Medieval
Bloomery

0 ——— ½ mile
0 ——— 500m

363 ▲

E n n e r d a l e   F e l l

DISTANCE	MINIMUM TIME	GRADIENT	LEVEL OF DIFFICULTY
2.5 miles (4km)	1hr	131ft (40m) ▲▲▲	✛✛✛

PATHS Forest paths and tracks
LANDSCAPE Woods, fell and lake
SUGGESTED MAP OS Explorer OL4 The English Lakes (NW)
START/FINISH Grid reference: NY 110153
DOG FRIENDLINESS A good walk for dogs
PARKING Bowness Knott car park
PUBLIC TOILETS None on route, nearest at Cleator Moor